Reader's Digest
Outdoor &
Garden DIY
Manual

0276 44082X 0829 81

Reader's Digest
Outdoor &
Garden DIY
Manual

Expert guidance on outdoor and garden DIY

Published by
The Reader's Digest Association Limited
London • New York • Sydney • Montreal

Contents

Your house and garden

Outdoor repairs

Roofs

Drainage

Walls and woodwork

DIY in the garden

Garden structures

Your House and Garden

Home survey

Carry out a survey on the outside of your house. You may be able to carry out any small repairs yourself. Consult a surveyor or building engineer if your survey alerts you to a serious problem, such as subsidence, that requires major structural work.

Start on the roof Start your home survey with the roof. A pair of binoculars is useful for inspecting it without having to climb a ladder. If you can't see the whole roof surface from your garden or the street, ask to view it from a neighbour's property.

Chimneys These are the most exposed part of your house, so check them closely for signs of damage. Start at the top of each stack, checking for cracks in the pots and in the mortar layer (flaunching) that holds them in place on the stack. Then inspect the brickwork and the pointing, noting any frost-damaged bricks or missing mortars. Consider having unused flues capped. Because of its position and the potential danger, few DIY jobs can be done on a chimney stack – special scaffolding must be erected around the stack so work can be done in safety. But keep an eye on the condition of the stack and have any repairs carried out quickly to prevent damp.

Leaks in the roof Discovering exactly where a pitched roof is leaking can be difficult. Rain can trickle down the roofing felt and then along the sides of rafters before it drips onto the loft floor. Look for clues such as dampness on a party wall or chimney stack in the loft, which might indicate that flashings are defective or missing (see page 31). Getting someone to play a hose on the roof, area by area, while you remain inside the loft can also help to reveal where the water is getting in.

Gutters and downpipes Check for blockages (see pages 36 and 39) which can cause gutters and downpipes to overflow. Stains on the house walls can reveal where previous overflows have occurred. Use a hosepipe to check where gutters are overflowing or where water is leaking from downpipe joints.

External woodwork Prod woodwork with a bradawl to detect rot under the paintwork and look round the edges of door and window frames for gaps where rainwater can penetrate – especially on north and west-facing walls, which are the most exposed to the weather.

Home security As you work your way around the house checking the woodwork, look at how windows and external doors are secured. You may need to fit new locks or upgrade existing ones.

Ventilation Airbricks or grilles are built into the outside walls, just above ground level, in houses with suspended timber ground floors. These allow air to circulate in the underfloor space, helping to keep it dry and to discourage rot. Make sure they are not blocked or obstructed in any way.

Signs of damp Patches of dampness on walls around windows and doors are usually caused by rain getting through gaps between their frames and the surrounding masonry. Where the damp is below the opening, it may be because there is no drip groove to stop the water creeping under a projecting sill or threshold. If there is a drip groove, make sure the rain is not crossing it because it is blocked with paint or mortar.

Subsidence This is the most serious problem you might detect in your property. It occurs most commonly on clay soil, which expands when wet and then contracts as it dries out. Look at the corners of your house and at the door and window openings. Are they vertical and square? Zigzag cracks running down the walls from the corners of door and window frames, and between the main house and an extension, are signs of possible subsidence. Inside the house, doors and windows may start jamming for no apparent reason, and wallpaper can crease or tear.

Rising damp Look for a damp-proof course (DPC) – visible outside between the second and third courses of brickwork above ground level. This is a horizontal band of slate, bituminous felt or black polythene (see page 49). In an older house built before DPCs were introduced, you may see a row of small mortar or rubber plugs indicating that a chemical DPC has been injected into the walls in recent years.

If you think you have rising damp in your house, make sure the DPC isn't covered by a flowerbed, path, drive or patio. Look for rendering that has been applied over the DPC. Curing these common causes of rising damp will solve the problem for little or no cost, saving you from incurring an expensive bill from a professional damp-proofing firm.

Garden features Remember to survey the garden at the same time as the rest of your home. Fences may be in poor condition, walls may need repairing, a shed roof may be leaking, garden paths may need lighting, and nearby trees may be undermining boundary walls. A gate or door into the garden might need a lock fitting to it.

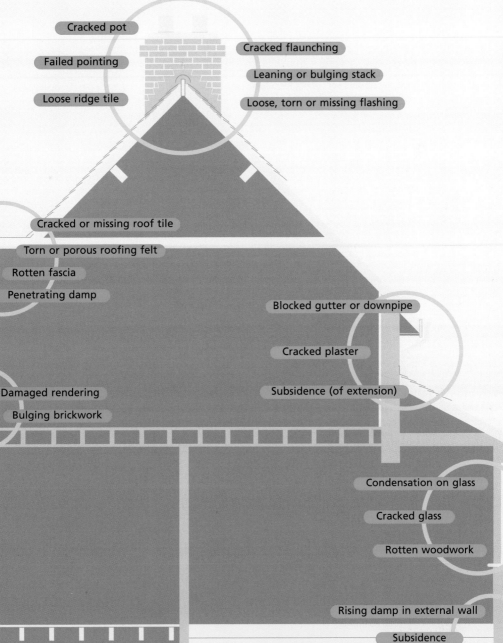

Cracked pot

Cracked flaunching

Failed pointing

Leaning or bulging stack

Loose ridge tile

Loose, torn or missing flashing

Cracked or missing roof tile

Torn or porous roofing felt

Rotten fascia

Penetrating damp

Blocked gutter or downpipe

Cracked plaster

Damaged rendering

Subsidence (of extension)

Bulging brickwork

Condensation on glass

Cracked glass

Rotten woodwork

Rising damp in external wall

Subsidence

What can go wrong on the roof

You may discover that the roof needs to be repaired only when stains appear on the ceiling from rain seeping into the loft.

Making regular checks in the loft for damp timber and checking the roof from the outside for signs of damage could help you to discover the problem earlier. Repair damage as soon as possible after its discovery.

To examine the roof thoroughly, set up a ladder which is at least three rungs above the gutter. If you move onto the roof, use a proper roof ladder which hooks over the ridge.

Flat roofs The main problem with a flat roof is that instead of draining off, water may collect on the surface and seep through even very small cracks. This can lead to rot in the timbers as well as damp patches appearing on ceilings.

Felt is generally built up in layers on larger roofs, and often the top layer will blister. To repair the damage, see page 32.

WHEN SHOULD A WHOLE ROOF BE REPLACED?

It is hard to judge whether a roof should be completely re-surfaced. If a large number of the tiles or slates are broken, this is obviously needed. Faults in the structure are harder to diagnose. Bumps and hollows may have been caused by movement in the roof timbers years earlier, but it may have stabilised and be perfectly sound and weatherproof. If movement is recent, however, it may need professional attention.

If you have doubts about the soundness of your roof, pay an architect or surveyor to give an unbiased report on it; a builder's report may not be so impartial.

Bitumen felt roofs on sheds are usually only a single sheet of felt. If this starts to break up, it should be stripped off and replaced. It is probably best to get a professional roofer to replace a flat roof.

Corrugated plastic sheeting may leak at overlaps or where screws or nails pass through the sheets. Seal any gaps with silicone sealant or replace the sheet (see page 33).

Glass roofing may leak if the seal fails along glazing bars and rain may be driven up overlaps by strong winds. Use adhesive tape – preferably the foil type, rather than

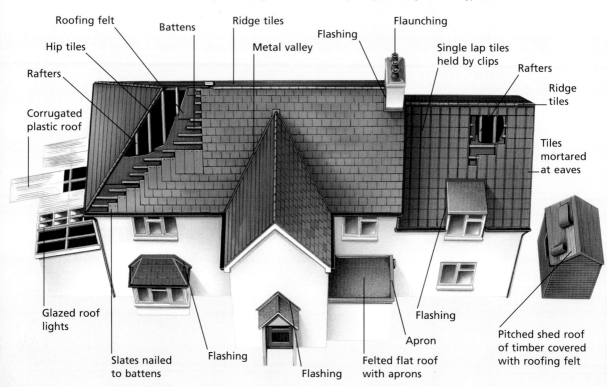

Roofing felt

Battens

Ridge tiles

Metal valley

Flashing

Flaunching

Hip tiles

Single lap tiles held by clips

Rafters

Rafters

Ridge tiles

Corrugated plastic roof

Tiles mortared at eaves

Glazed roof lights

Flashing

Apron

Pitched shed roof of timber covered with roofing felt

Slates nailed to battens

Flashing

Flashing

Felted flat roof with aprons

the black – to seal a glazing bar. If a poor overlap cannot be increased, seal the outer gap with silicone sealant.

Ridge tiles Most houses have ridge and hip tiles set in a continuous mortar bed, and when this cracks up the tiles can be dislodged by high winds, allowing water to get in and rot the timbers. Check that yours are all secure, and identify any loose ones with a chalk cross so they can be lifted and re-bedded securely. To replace a ridge tile, see page 27.

Roof tiles Tiles are usually nailed in place or held by the nibs that project behind each tile and hook over roofing battens. If the nibs are damaged or if the nails rust away, tiles will slide down the roof. Tiles may also be blown off by strong winds or pushed out of place by the weight of a build-up of snow that turns to ice. To replace a roof tile, see page 23.

Slates There are no nibs on slates, so they need nails to hold them. They may slip out of position if the nails rust. To replace a slate, see page 26.

Flashings When a roof surface meets a wall or chimney stack, the gap between them is sealed with flashing. Lead or aluminium flashing is the most durable type; felt and mortar flashings do not last quite as long.

Make sure the upper edges of flashings are held securely in the mortar between the bricks, and that their lower edges lie flat on the roof; if they're not, rain can get behind and the roof will leak. Flashings can become displaced when mortar joints fail (the flashing strip is pushed into the joint between bricks or pieces of masonry and sealed with mortar). Cracked mortar flashing is usually caused by slight movement in the building or between neighbouring buildings. This movement is common and depends on the water content in the soil.

For how to repair flashings, see page 31. Check all the flashings – around chimney stacks, dormer windows and adjoining flat roofs – when making a repair. Replace mortar fillets with metal flashings because mortar cracks.

Chimney stacks If a flue is not in use, rain which gets onto the flue lining can cause damp problems. Have the chimney capped with a half-round tile or a cowl to keep rain out. You can only see the edge of the flaunching (the mortar which holds the pots in place) but have it checked if any

deterioration is visible. If you notice any faults in the brickwork, you should get expert advice.

If a stack is built against an outside wall, examine it for straightness. The combination of coal gases condensing inside the flue and rain soaking through the mortar joints can set up a chemical reaction which makes the brickwork bulge outwards. Repointing the brickwork and lining the flue can arrest the problem, but a severely damaged stack may have to be completely rebuilt.

Valleys Valleys – the internal angles where two roof slopes meet – are usually lined with a metal tray secured to wooden boards that are themselves supported by the roof rafters. Keep them clear of wind-blown debris so they can't overflow and soak the woodwork. Check them for splits or tears too; any you find can be waterproofed temporarily by sticking on some self-adhesive flashing tape. See page 30 for repairs to metal valleys.

Verges At gables, the end tiles of each row may project beyond the face of the wall to form what is known as a verge. This overhang is supported on plain tiles, slates or strips of fibre cement sheet bedded on top of the sloping masonry. Check that the mortar forming the verge is intact. If it's cracked or missing, high winds could lift and dislodge the tiles. See page 29 for repairs to verges.

Test an old slate by tapping it lightly with a hammer. You'll hear a ringing sound if it's in good condition, and a dull sound if it's cracked. Look at the underside, too; it's usually the first surface to powder and crumble.

What can go wrong with the house exterior

Check the outside of your house on a regular basis. Even minor problems, such as blocked gutters, can cause serious problems if left untreated.

Cladding Timber cladding, which forms part of an exterior wall, must be protected by preservative or paint if it is not to be affected by damp, otherwise wet rot may set in. Test the wood by prodding it with a sharp screwdriver or knife. If the wood is soft and pulpy, it needs treatment. Plastic cladding is not affected by damp but gaps surrounding the cladding must be tightly sealed. Seal any gaps round window frames using frame sealant.

Brick walls Facing brick naturally absorbs a certain amount of rainwater, which penetrates partly into the wall. When the weather dries up, the moisture evaporates and no harm is done. In older houses, some bricks may have become over porous so that they do not dry completely. This could lead to damp penetrating indoors.

External walls Rain beating upon an external wall will be partially absorbed, causing damp to appear. Water from a dripping overflow pipe from a WC cistern may splash onto a wall.

Damp masonry can be damaged by frost, which freezes water within the wall structure and makes it expand, splitting the faces off bricks and detaching rendering from the masonry.

Salts in the bricks may react with rainwater, producing a white powdery deposit called efflorescence (see page 44). This is common on new brick walls.

Faults in a damp-proof course (DPC) may allow water to rise from the ground and soak the wall (see page 49). Soil heaped over a DPC can also cause damp.

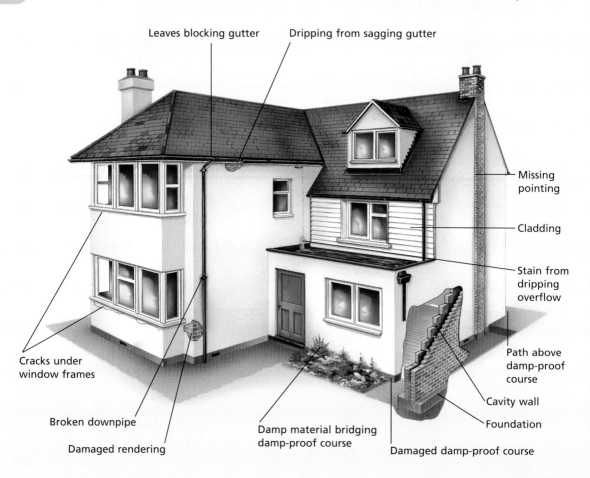

Leaves blocking gutter

Dripping from sagging gutter

Missing pointing

Cladding

Stain from dripping overflow

Path above damp-proof course

Cavity wall

Foundation

Cracks under window frames

Broken downpipe

Damaged rendering

Damp material bridging damp-proof course

Damaged damp-proof course

Defective pointing will allow water to penetrate the outer leaf (the outer skin of bricks). For repointing, see page 44.

Excessive damp in an external wall should be dealt with as soon as possible before it can damage the interior. You can usually see the damp patch because the wet brickwork or masonry is a different colour from the dry parts.

Window and door frames If there are gaps around window and door frames the rain may soak between the masonry and the frame and rot will set into the timber. You should dig out the worst of the rot and apply a combination of wood repairing products, such as a liquid wood hardener, high-performance wood filler and wood preservative pellets before priming and repainting the wood. Also maintain the paintwork (pages 53–55) to prevent rot.

Renderings Cracks and gaps in a rendered surface may allow damp to penetrate and be held in the wall. In extreme cases, this can lead to blisters which must be cut away before the rendering is repaired. For repairing cracks, and patching rendering, see pages 44–47.

Gutters A gutter may leak at the joints between sections; it may become blocked and overflow; or it may sag so that water does not run away properly. In each case water may soak into the wall and penetrate to the inside, causing damp and damage to the decoration. Even on a cavity wall, water may find a way from the outer to the inner leaf of brickwork.

Cast-iron gutter sections are usually sealed with putty at joints and bolted together. The putty may disintegrate in time and, in extreme cases, bolts may rust and drop out. A plastic gutter may leak because the clip which seals two sections together has become loose, or because the neoprene gasket has perished, or because the gutter has an incorrect fall, and water spills over.

Sometimes screws holding gutter brackets to the fascia board rust away or the fascia board itself might rot, causing the brackets to move and the gutter sections to sag. For cleaning, aligning and repairing roof gutters, see pages 35–38.

Downpipes The most common problem with downpipes is that they become blocked – and if they (or the gutters leading to them) overflow or leak, damp may start in the walls.

Most downpipes first get blocked at the top and then are often obstructed farther down as the blockage sinks down the pipe

under pressure of rain. For information on clearing blockages, see page 39.

Cast-iron pipes may crack if damp material stuck inside freezes. When they thaw the pipes will leak and the leaks may cause damage.

Cavity walls Houses built since about 1920 have cavity walls – developed as a way to prevent damp penetrating solid wall structures. Early examples have two brick walls (known as leaves) separated by an open cavity and held together by metal wall ties. Newer houses have the inner cavity leaf (and the outer one too if the exterior is rendered or has tiling or weatherboarding) built of insulating blockwork rather than brickwork to reduce heat losses.

Problems arise with cavity walls when the wall ties which link the outer and inner leaves are bridged by a mortar dropped during construction of the house. It acts as a wick, carrying moisture across the cavity to the interior wall. Cavity walls should be free of all damp before you have the cavity insulated. Treating the external face of the wall with a silicone water repellent will cure the damp.

Mortar between bricks may become highly porous and carry water into the wall. This fault often becomes apparent after a freeze – as the water expands, it breaks up the mortar, which will crumble and fall out of joints. For how to repair the damage, see page 44.

Clear out your gutters using a gutter scoop. You can make one by cutting the bottom from a suitably shaped plastic motor-oil container. Use the spout as a handle – it will hold much more than a garden trowel.

Garden survey

For most of us, the chance to design a garden from scratch happens only once or twice in a lifetime. Whether you have a virgin plot or want to make radical changes to an established garden, it's worth making a proper plan.

Garden features

All gardens include structural features – some practical, such as a shed or a patio, and others of aesthetic value, like a pond, planting beds or a pergola. They need to be juggled successfully into a new layout, so list the features you want in order of priority and plan in your essentials first, so that the layout is not compromised by having to accommodate too many features.

Patios and paved areas make a great focus for relaxing, entertaining and eating outside, as well as being a level space for children to play. Paving slabs create a hard-wearing surface for a flat area, while timber decking is excellent for sloping sites or a garden on different levels. A patio is usually adjacent to the house for convenience, but you could site it elsewhere to take advantage of sun, shelter or a view. If there is space, you could have more than one patio to enjoy the sun at different times of day. To construct a patio see pages 88–95.

Paths are a key part of a garden. They link different areas and lead you around the garden. They are usually surfaced with paving, gravel or stepping stones. To lay a path see pages 88–90.

A lawn is not compulsory, though it remains a traditional choice, especially if you have children. For those who wish to give up the regular chore of mowing, and especially in small gardens or where the grass is overshadowed or quickly gets worn, alternatives do exist. Consider materials such as paving slabs, bricks, paviors, timber decking, granite setts, gravel or slate chippings. Chipped bark can provide a soft surface for a children's play area. Bear in mind that the ground surfaces of a garden set an overall style, in much the same way as choice of flooring affects the look of a room.

Beds and borders provide the growing space for your selection of plants. The choice is very personal, but with the variety now available it is possible to have plants of interest throughout the year.

Boundaries create shelter and privacy. Plan new boundaries as an integral part of the garden's design. Check out materials to see what would work best in your area. To build a fence or wall see pages 73–83 and 100–107.

Vertical structures create visual interest as well as extra growing space. They might include a pergola to cast dappled shade over a sunny patio; an arbour for a secluded seat; arches over gates and paths; trellis or screens to divide up the garden; or obelisks for climbing plants. To construct a pergola or arbour see pages 62–66.

A pond or water feature can be made to any size and design to suit the garden. Moving water generally requires access to electricity. To create a pond or water feature see pages 112–117.

Lighting aids security and allows greater use of the garden at night in summer. Unless solar-powered lights are used, access to electricity is needed. See page 118 for varieties of outdoor lights.

Conservatory: if you think you may want to add one at a later date, make a note to allow sufficient space in the design.

A garden shed is essential for a storing a lawn mower, tools, garden furniture and bicycles. To build a shed see page 70.

A greenhouse is an essential item for plant enthusiasts. It should be sited in an open position to take full avantage of sunlight. To erect a greenhouse see pages 68–69.

HELPFUL TIPS

• Dividing a garden into separate areas, each with a distinct character, can work well in all but very small plots. If you do not see the whole garden at a glance, you are encouraged to step out and explore.
• Screening off dark or awkward corners allows you to hide a shed, compost heap or dustbins behind planting, trellis or willow hurdles.

Planning a new garden

Faced with the prospect of a complete garden makeover, some people hire a garden designer. But it could be more fun – as well as more challenging and satisfying – to do it yourself. First, focus your thoughts by writing down what you want from your garden. Think carefully about how you and your family will use it, day to day. Do you like eating outdoors? Do you want a children's play area? Must you have a shed? For inspiration, look at other people's gardens, and garden design books and magazines that show a range of solutions for different shapes and sizes of garden. Visit plant nurseries for ideas about plants, features and materials.

Assess what you have Next, carry out a critical assessment of what you actually have in your plot or existing garden. Take your time over this important stage as you may find you have many plants and materials worth saving. Try to allow a full year before you finalise your plans, so you can see what plants are growing in different parts of the garden, and how they perform season by season.

The soil has a great influence on which plants can be grown. Both the soil pH (its level of acidity or alkalinity) and its type can vary enormously from place to place,

so it is a good idea to test the soil in different parts of your garden at this stage of the process.

Re-using plants and materials If you inherit well-established plants, they can give the garden a sense of maturity. Neglected plants will need rejuvenating by renovation pruning – or they may have to be taken out altogether. Try to identify those you are considering keeping. Materials can be recycled too. For example, good-quality paving slabs from an unwanted patio can be used for a path, while cheap concrete slabs will make a good base for a new shed or greenhouse.

Orientation, sun and shade Use a compass to find north and ascertain the aspect of different parts of the garden. Take into account the shade cast by large trees and by neighbouring buildings, and do not grow sun-loving plants there. Remember that in summer the sun is high in the sky, reducing the amount of shade cast in winter.

Make an initial sketch Start by drawing a rough sketch of your existing garden (below). Note which areas are sunny or shady at different times of day and year. For planting, note which spots are sheltered and warm, or cold and exposed: plants vary in their preferences for growing conditions.

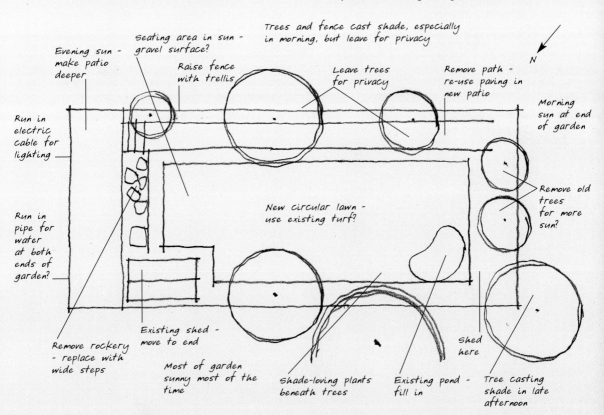

Seating area in sun – gravel surface?

Evening sun – make patio deeper

Raise fence with trellis

Trees and fence cast shade, especially in morning, but leave for privacy

Leave trees for privacy

Remove path – re-use paving in new patio

N

Morning sun at end of garden

Run in electric cable for lighting

Remove old trees for more sun?

Run in pipe for water at both ends of garden?

New circular lawn – use existing turf?

Remove rockery – replace with wide steps

Existing shed – move to end

Most of garden sunny most of the time

Shade-loving plants beneath trees

Existing pond – fill in

Shed here

Tree casting shade in late afternoon

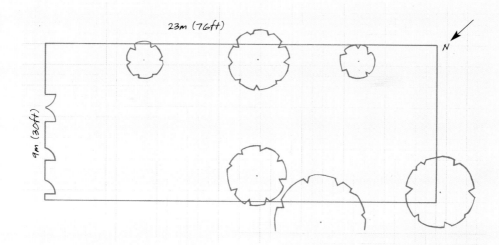

23m (76ft)

9m (30ft)

N

Draw up an accurate plan Planning your garden on paper enables you to correct potential mistakes before they become a reality. The drawing must be to scale in order to get an accurate picture of the layout. A scale of 2cm = 1m is good for most gardens, or 1cm = 2ft if working in imperial measures. You will need a long tape measure, a piece of paper for the outline sketch, graph paper and tracing paper, pencil, ruler, rubber and a pair of compasses for drawing circles.

Working outdoors:
• Make an outline sketch of your plot.
• Measure the site down the centre, starting from the house and working outwards. Note down all measurements and distances between key features.
• Indicate all existing features that you want to keep, such as paving, paths and garden buildings, as well as plants.
• Make a note of anything outside the garden that influences your plot, such as a tree overhanging from next door.
• Indicate north on the sketch.

Indoors, at your leisure:
• On graph paper, use your measurements to make a scale drawing (see above) of the outline of your garden and retained features.
• Secure a sheet of tracing paper over the outline, and sketch on your new layout (see opposite). This allows you to do several different versions of the layout, without spoiling your scale outline.
• You could cut out and label 'footprints' of larger features, like garden buildings, on card so you can move them around on your plan before finally siting them.

The family garden

The garden illustrated here is designed for a family with growing children and takes into account their need for safe play areas and soft surfaces. The rectangular plot has been divided into three areas, giving a large paved patio near the house on which children can play, in view of the kitchen window, and an area behind the main lawn for a climbing frame and swing.

In between, a gravelled patio takes advantage of a sunny spot on which to sit and eat outdoors, while the circular lawn gives a soft surface for activities from sunbathing to ball games. The shed is sited behind the lawn, screened off by climbers and shrubs, while the dustbin store is conveniently near the back door.

Advantage has been taken of a sloping site to introduce a change of level and a visual break part way up the garden, with steps up to the gravelled patio. Some trees have been retained, to give the garden a sense of maturity, and shrubs on the boundary have also been kept, to help block out the view of buildings beyond.

Mixed borders soften boundaries and allow the adults to indulge an interest in plants, with a herb bed and children's own 'garden' area close to the kitchen.

A finished scheme

All successful gardens cater for the interests of the owners, but the best designs have the flexibility to allow for changing priorities. We have designed this garden to provide safe play areas for children and for adults to enjoy the garden too. But you can easily adapt your garden for different uses.

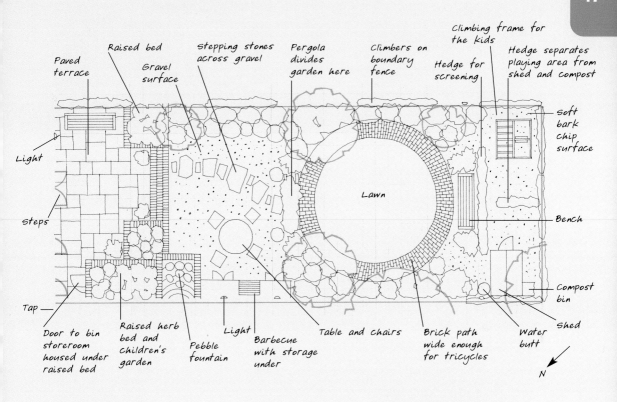

Paved terrace

Raised bed

Gravel surface

stepping stones across gravel

Pergola divides garden here

Climbers on boundary fence

Climbing frame for the kids

Hedge for screening

Hedge separates playing area from shed and compost

Soft bark chip surface

Light

Lawn

Bench

steps

Compost bin

Tap

Shed

Water butt

N

Door to bin storeroom housed under raised bed

Raised herb bed and children's garden

Pebble fountain

Light

Barbecue with storage under

Table and chairs

Brick path wide enough for tricycles

Family garden

Paving slabs and slate make comfortable stepping stones across the area of gravel.

A lawn is everyone's play space. For a new lawn, use turf or a seed mixture that will stand up to lots of use.

A play area for older children is sited at the end of the garden on a surface of bark chips, and partially screened from view.

A sizeable patio provides a safe space for young children to play in full view of the house. This one has room for toys, a paddling pool or even a sandpit.

Shallow steps lead from the patio to the eating area, dividing the garden and introducing a deliberate change of level into a sloping site.

Herbs are handy for both kitchen and barbecue.

A bubble fountain is a soothing water feature and a safe option where there are young children in the family.

The barbecue is situated next to the table and chairs for alfresco meals.

The wide brick path running around the lawn makes a great tricycle and skate track.

General safety

Follow these precautions to keep yourself safe when you are carrying out DIY jobs outdoors.

Use tools safely

Many DIY tools need sharp blades or powerful motors to be able to do their jobs properly. This means that they can cause injury if they are not used correctly and with care. When using bladed tools, keep them sharp so they will cut without effort, and make sure that your hands are behind the cutting direction and out of the cutting line. Read the instructions before using any power tool for the first time, and never bypass or de-activate any safety guard that is fitted to the tool.

Wear the right safety gear

Assemble a safety kit before embarking on DIY work. For many outdoor jobs, you will need a hard hat, a pair of strong work gloves and sturdy footwear. You should also have safety goggles, a face mask and, if you intend to use noisy power tools for long periods, some ear protectors too. For work on the roof, a tool pouch ensures you have both hands free and reduces the chances of tools sliding down the roof.

Power tools in the garden

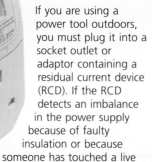

If you are using a power tool outdoors, you must plug it into a socket outlet or adaptor containing a residual current device (RCD). If the RCD detects an imbalance in the power supply because of faulty insulation or because someone has touched a live part, the RCD will switch off the supply immediately – fast enough to prevent an electric shock from being fatal.

Carrying heavy loads

Take care when lifting heavy items such as large paving slabs. So you don't injure yourself, stand close to whatever you're lifting with your feet apart and your back straight. Squat down so you can grip the load. Then straighten your legs and stand up as you lift the load, keeping it as close to your body as possible. If something is too heavy or awkward to lift alone, get help or look into the range of lifting equipment that can be hired. This includes items such as panel lifters, barrows for carting flagstones around the garden, and manual grabs for handling bricks.

New wiring regulations

Since January 2005, all new domestic wiring work in England and Wales must comply with the requirements of a new section of the Building Regulations. Part P, entitled Electrical Safety, covers design, installation, inspection and testing of electrical work in the home. It applies to both professional and DIY electrical work.

If you install any new outdoor circuit, such as one supplying garden lighting or an outbuilding, you must notify your local authority building control department before you start work. When the job is completed the local authority will inspect and test your work for a fee of around £100-£200. They will then issue you with a Building Regulations Self-certification Certificate and an Electrical Installation Certificate. If you are in any doubt as to whether the work you plan to do requires notification, contact your local authority building control department for advice.

Safety on the rooftop

Have a helper to hand When you are working at a height make sure you have a helper with you. Ask them to steady the weight at the bottom of the ladder when you are carrying up heavy items.

Have a safe place to put your tools Fix a tray to a ladder or hold tools in a bag or pouch slung across your chest, or wear a tool belt.

Lower debris to the ground Use a stout sack or bucket attached to a rope to lower anything to the ground. Take care not to drop anything; it could cause serious injury.

Using ladders safely

Secure a firm foothold If a ladder is going to be in one position for a lengthy job, tie it to sturdy pegs driven into the ground on each side of the uprights to prevent it slipping. On hard surfaces, or when you need to move the ladder frequently, get someone to stand on the bottom rung of the ladder and anchor it in place.

On soft ground, stand the ladder on a board to stop it from sinking. Screw a batten to the board to prevent the ladder from sliding outwards, then tie and stake it. Alternatively, you can hire a ladder safety foot, which has a high-friction base.

With the ladder set up, climb three rungs and jump up and down, then lean out to each side to check that it won't settle. Reposition the ladder on firmer ground or on a board if it moves.

One of the most useful accessories for improving ladder safety is a safety foot, which can be bought or hired. The high-friction base resists slipping when the ladder is standing on a hard surface. It also spreads the load and stops the feet of the ladder from sinking into soft ground.

Get a good grip Hold the rungs, not the ladder sides, when you climb or descend a ladder. If you miss your footing, you will automatically grab them and so avoid a fall. If you hold the sides and you slip, you will get skin burns from a metal ladder and splinters from a wooden one. Don't hug the ladder; climb with your arms straight and your body upright.

Stand well away Fit a stand-off to the top of your ladder to hold it away from overhanging eaves and allow you to work on the gutters. You may crack a plastic gutter if you rest a ladder against it.

Change to cordless Power cables hanging from ladders are a potential safety hazard; use cordless power tools whenever you can.

Don't climb too high Use the top four rungs of a ladder as handholds only. If you try to stand on them and grab something higher up for support, such as a gutter or sill, you are quite likely to fall.

Outdoor repairs and maintenance

Roof repairs: tools for the job

It is possible to make minor repairs to your roof, but you should always have a helper and be safety-conscious when working at height.

Roof ladder Never venture onto a roof without a purpose-made roof ladder fitted at one end with rubber wheels and a large hook. Using the wheels, you can push the ladder up the roof without dislodging slates or tiles. When the top of the ladder reaches the roof ridge, turn it over so that the hook lodges on the ridge securely. The ladder must reach all the way from the roof ridge to the gutter to allow you to transfer easily from the ordinary ladder on which you have climbed to gutter level. Extension pieces can be added to a roof ladder if necessary.

Hire a roof ladder rather than buy one; or buy the wheels-and-hook section for fitting onto a conventional ladder.

Scaffold towers If you have to work all along the gutter, hire a scaffold tower with locking wheels, guard rail and a firm platform.

Ladders Always make sure that the ladder is set up at the correct angle: 1m away from the wall for every 4m up the wall.

The ladder or scaffold tower should be long enough or high enough to reach at least 600mm beyond the working point to avoid the need to stretch.

Fit a stand-off bracket to the top of a ladder to make sure it presses against the wall, not against an insecure gutter.

For extra security, you can screw an eye bolt into the fascia board and tie the ladder to it. Always move the ladder or scaffold tower along the wall to take you within easy reach of the working point. Never lean sideways to reach the work.

Plugging chisel The plugging chisel, also called a seam chisel, is designed to remove mortar from between bricks or pieces of masonry. It can be used when replacing flashing. The fluted face of the blade allows debris to be cleared quickly and easily.

Slate cutter When the handles are squeezed together, the steel blades meet and shear off the edge of the slate. Useful for cutting an oversized slate to the right size.

Tinsnips The scissor-action will cut through lead, zinc or other sheet metals used for roof valleys. Snips are made in several sizes – from 200–360mm long.

Slate ripper The steel blade is about 280–380mm long. It is slipped under the tile or slate to be removed until one of the barbs of its arrow-shaped tip can be hooked round a nail that is driven into the roof batten. A sharp tug, or a hammer blow on the curve of the handle, jerks the barb down, and it cuts through the nail. The ripper is then moved to the other edge of the tile or slate to cut the second nail.

Slate rippers can be hired.

Soft-faced mallet A mallet with a head made of rubber, plastic or rawhide is used to tap sheet metal into shape – when renewing a valley, for example.

Roof repairs

Missing or broken slates or tiles can allow water to penetrate the roof space and wind to lift off neighbouring tiles. Act promptly to fix the problem.

Making a temporary repair to a cracked tile or slate

If rainwater is coming in through a cracked tile or slate and it is not possible to get a replacement immediately, you can use flashing strip to make a temporary repair to minimise the damage done by damp. Alternatively, bituminous sealant in an applicator gun seals a fine crack with very little work: prop up the surrounding tiles and brush the crack as for flashing strip, and then inject the sealant.

Tools *Ladder with a stand-off bracket; roof ladder; wooden wedges (see box, right); wire brush; paintbrush; sharp knife; old wallpaper seam roller.*

Materials *Flashing strip primer; self-adhesive flashing strip.*

1 Raise the one or two tiles or slates that overlap the cracked one, to give you better access. Prop them up with small wooden wedges (see right). Use the wire brush to clean the surface round the crack.

2 Brush a coat of flashing strip primer into and round the crack, making a strip as wide as the flashing strip. The primer ensures a good bond between tile or slate and flashing strip.

3 Cut a piece of flashing strip from the roll with a sharp knife. Make it long enough to cover the whole crack.

4 Press the strip into place and bed it down well. Run a small wallpaper seam roller to and fro over it to firm it down.

Replacing a broken plain tile

If you don't have a spare tile of the same size and style as the broken one, a builders' yard or salvage merchant may have one or be able to obtain one for you.

Before you start Beware of matching the replacement tile to the colour your tiles were when new. The tiles may have changed colour considerably, so try to match the replacement to the colour they are now. If you can't find a good match, 'steal' a tile from an unobtrusive place on the roof – such as a side porch. A tile near the end of the bottom course will be easy to reach. Put the poor match in its place.

Tools *Ladder with stand-off bracket; roof ladder; wooden wedges; large builder's trowel. Perhaps a slate ripper.*

Materials *Replacement tile.*

WEDGES TO PROP TILES UP

To prop up tiles you need to prepare two or more wedges from 20mm thick wood. Cut them 200mm long and make them taper from 30mm at one end to a point at the other.

---

1 Lift the two tiles that overlap the broken tile from the course above. Tap a wooden wedge under each to hold it up.

2 Slip the large builder's trowel under the broken tile. Lift up the whole tile until its nibs are clear of the batten and you can draw it out towards you.

Alternatively If the broken tile is one that has been nailed to the batten, try to free it by wiggling it from side to side until the nail breaks or comes away.

If this does not free it, you will have to use a slate ripper (page 22) to cut through the nails. Slate rippers can be hired.

3 Lay the replacement tile on the trowel and slide it up under the two wedged tiles until the nibs hook over the batten. There is no need to nail it, even if the original was nailed. Take out the wedges.

Replacing a group of plain tiles

If you need to replace a group of tiles and have no spares, buy replacements of the same size and style. See advice for a single tile (see page 23).

Tools *Ladder with stand-off bracket; roof ladder; wooden wedges (page 23); large builder's trowel; claw hammer; bucket on a long rope. Perhaps a slate ripper.*

Materials *Replacement tiles; 40mm aluminium-alloy roofing nails.*

1 Lift the tiles in the course immediately above the highest ones to be replaced. Lift them two at a time and slide the wooden wedges under their outer edges to hold them up. This will allow you access to the tile they overlap in the course below.

2 As each tile is exposed, slide the trowel under it and lift it until its nibs clear the batten. Then draw it out. Lower it to the ground in the bucket.

If a tile is nailed to the batten, see-saw it from side to side to try to dislodge the nails. If you cannot, use a slate ripper (page 22) to cut through the nails.

3 Work along the top course of tiles to be removed and then along the course below that, and so on until all the tiles have been removed. Once the highest course of tiles has been removed, you can lift the others without using the wedges or the trowel.

4 Fit the replacement tiles onto the battens along the bottom course first. Hook each tile over the batten by its nibs and make sure that it is centred over the gap between the two tiles below it. Then work along the courses above.

5 Nail each tile in every third or fourth course to the batten with two nails.

6 To fit the top course, hold up the tiles in the course above in pairs with wedges. Work along the row, lifting each new tile on the trowel and sliding it into place.

Replacing broken single lap tiles

Tools *Ladder with a stand-off bracket; roof ladder; wooden wedges (page 23). Perhaps a slate ripper; hammer; bucket on a rope.*

Materials *Replacement tiles. Perhaps tile clips and 40mm roofing aluminium-alloy roofing nails.*

1 Slide up the tiles that overlap onto the broken tile. Alternatively, use wedges to raise the tiles to the left and right of the broken one, but in the course above.

2 To remove the broken tile, tilt it sideways to separate it from the tiles which are interlocked with it. You will be able to free it without disturbing them. Lever the tile upwards to release it from any clip that holds it to the batten. If the clip stays in place, the new tile may slip into it. If the clip is dislodged, there is no need to replace it; a few unclipped tiles will not matter. Sometimes alternate courses are nailed in place. If your repair is to a nailed tile, use a slate ripper to cut the nails before you remove the tile.

3 Lower the broken tile in a bucket on a rope to a helper on the ground.

4 To fit the replacement tile, slide it up into place. You will not be able to nail it or clip it. Pull back into place any tiles that you pushed out of place. Remove any wedges.

Replacing a group of tiles

Remove the highest tiles as for a single tile. Lower tiles simply need tilting to free them. Remove the clips wherever you can.

When replacing the tiles, fit the lowest course first and work from right to left. Fit a clip for each tile wherever you are able to nail it to the batten.

Lodge the hook of the clip over the ridge at the side of the tile and hammer the nail through the hole in the clip into the top edge of the batten near the bottom edge of the tile you are fitting.

You can also nail alternate courses to the battens. The highest course cannot be nailed and the last tile of all cannot be fitted with a clip because the batten will be covered.

Making repairs to slate roofs

Slates will last a century or more, but the nails holding them to battens can corrode and break, allowing the slates to slip out of position.

Before you start The two problems most likely to affect a slate roof are nail-sickness and delamination. Corrosion, or nail-sickness, can affect a large area of a roof within a few years as the nails are the same age and corrode at the same rate. The slates can be re-nailed provided that they are sound.

A more serious problem is delamination, when the surface of the slate becomes flaky or powdery and you can see many cracks and splits. Replacement is the usual solution.

Fixing slates For fixing a group of replacement slates in several courses you can use 40mm aluminium-alloy or copper roofing nails.

If these are hard to find and you only have a small group of slates to nail into place, 40mm large-head galvanised clout nails will do.

CUTTING A SLATE TO SIZE

Place the slate on a flat board and use a ceramic tile cutter and a metal rule to score a deep cutting line. To complete the cut, use a wide bolster chisel. Tap it along the scored line with gentle hammer blows. Or you can place the slate on a table with the scored line over the table edge and press down to break the slate cleanly.

If you have many slates to cut, hire a slate cutter. Cut with the top surface of the slate downwards. On a second-hand slate in particular this ensures that weathering and cutting marks match the other slates. Alternatively, you can hire an electric tile cutter.

When you are replacing single slates, you will not be able to nail them because the batten will be covered by the course of slates above. You can secure each slate with a strip of metal cut from lead, zinc, or aluminium that is thin enough to bend. It is fixed between the slates (see right).

Slates can also be fixed with adhesive expanding foam, which can be applied under a loose slate from outside, or (if the slate is visible) from inside the loft.

How to make holes New slates will not have fixing holes in them; you will have to make the holes.

A secondhand slate may have its holes in the wrong place and need drilling. Use the old slate as a pattern to mark drilling spots. The holes are usually about half-way down the sides.

Drill the holes with an electric drill fitted with a No. 6 masonry bit; or make the hole by tapping a nail through the slate with steady, not-too-hard hammer blows.

Work from the underside, that is the side without the bevelled edges.

Replacing a broken slate

Slates may become cracked with age, or by someone clambering on the roof without using proper access equipment.

Before you start You may not be able to obtain a matching replacement slate immediately. If so, make a temporary repair to prevent water from penetrating. You can make it as for a tile (page 23).

Alternatively, you can coat the slate with mastic. Cover this with a piece of roofing felt or cooking foil cut to fit and spread another layer of mastic on top.

Replace the slate when you can obtain one that is a good match.

Tools *Ladder with a stand-off bracket; roof ladder; slate ripper; a bucket on a long rope; hammer or screwdriver. Perhaps a power drill fitted with No. 6 masonry bit, or nail and hammer.*

Materials *Replacement slate; strip of lead, zinc, aluminium or copper 25mm wide, and long enough to reach from the hole in the slate to the bottom plus 100mm; 40mm large-head galvanised clout nails.*

---

1 Cut through the nails that are holding the slate, using the slate ripper.

2 Draw the slate towards you, wiggling it from side to side to ease it from under the slates overlapping it. Take care not to let any broken pieces slide off the roof. They are sharp and can cause damage or injury. Put the pieces in a bucket and take it to the ground or lower it down to a helper.

3 Nail the metal strip to the batten, which will just be visible in the gap between the two slates the replacement is going to lap onto. Put the nail in a ready-made hole about 25mm down from the top of the strip.

4 Carry the new slate up to the roof in a bucket or put it into a bucket and haul it up with a rope.

5 Slip the new slate, with bevelled edges upwards, under the two slates in the course above. Wiggle it a little to right and left to work it upwards until its lower edge aligns with the slates on each side. Its top edge will fit tightly over the batten to which the course above is nailed.

6 Turn up the end of the metal strip over the lower edge of the slate, then bend it double and press it down flat against the slate. The double thickness prevents snow and ice from forcing the clip open.

Replacing a group of slates

You will be able to nail the lower courses of slates in place, but the top course and the course below that will have to be fixed with metal strips because the battens to which they should be nailed will be covered by slates (see Replacing a broken slate, opposite). If necessary, cut the slates to size and drill holes in them.

Tools *Ladder with a stand-off bracket; roof ladder; slate ripper (see page 22); hammer; a bucket on a long rope; screwdriver.*

Materials *Replacement slates; 40mm aluminium-alloy or copper roofing nails; strips of lead, zinc, aluminium or copper 25mm wide and long enough to reach from the hole in the slate to the bottom plus 100mm.*

1 Cut through the nails securing the damaged slates, using a slate ripper. Deal first with the highest course to be removed. Ease each slate out in turn from the overlapping slates and lower it in a bucket to a helper or take it to the ground. Do not let a slate slide from the roof; it is sharp and can cause damage or injury.

Work down course by course, removing the slates. The lower ones will not be overlapped and are easier to remove.

2 Fix the bottom course of replacement slates first. Butt neighbouring slates closely and fit them with the bevelled edges upwards. Nail the slates through the holes to the batten.

3 Work upwards, course by course, nailing the slates in place. When you can no longer see the battens to nail the slates to, cut metal strips to secure the slates and fit them as described in Replacing a broken slate (opposite).

Replacing ridge, hip and bonnet tiles

Both tiled and slate roofs have the gaps at the ridge and hips covered by specially designed tiles. The tiles are most often curved, but may be angled.

Replacing a bonnet hip tile

Some tiled roofs have bonnet hip tiles to cover the gap at the hip. Bonnet hip tiles are nailed to the hip timber as well as being bedded in mortar.

1 Remove a bonnet hip tile by chipping away the mortar above and below it with a cold chisel and club hammer and then sliding a slate ripper under the tile and giving a sharp hammer blow on the handle to cut through the nail. You can then draw out the tile towards you.

If you are removing several tiles down the hip, start at the highest one and work downwards. Clean the tiles of old mortar.

2 Brush away all dust from around the repair, then brush the area with water and with PVA adhesive.

3 If you are replacing a single tile, spread mortar to bed it on. Spread mortar also under the bonnet in the course above. Set the bonnet in place and tap it into alignment with the other tiles in the course before you smooth the mortar and clean away any excess.

4 If you are replacing several bonnets, work from the bottom upwards. Nail each, except the top one, to the timber with an aluminium nail after you have set it on the mortar. Then smooth the mortar and clean away any excess.

Replacing ridge or hip tiles

The most common problem at the roof ridge or hip is that the mortar between tiles cracks and crumbles away. Sometimes a tile may then be pushed out of place by a build-up of ice, or occasionally by strong winds. If you spot cracks early, while they are narrow, you can fill them with roof-and-gutter sealant. There are coloured sealants which make the repair scarcely noticeable.

If the mortar is crumbling or the tile itself has cracked, you will have to remove the tile and re-fix it or put a new one in its place. If it is the end ridge tile that needs a repair, you must seal up the opening left at the end. Use small pieces of slate or tile bedded in mortar. If the main roof tiles are S-shaped there will be a hollow to seal where the ridge or hip tile meets them.

Tools *Ladder with a stand-off bracket; roof ladder; cold chisel; club hammer; brush; paintbrush; small builder's trowel.*

Materials *Dry mortar mix, or cement and sharp sand; PVA adhesive; bucket of water. Perhaps replacement tiles, narrow pieces of tile or slate.*

1 With the chisel and hammer, carefully chip away all cracked or crumbling mortar until the ridge or hip tile is freed and you can lift it off. Make sure that any surrounding mortar you leave in place is sound. Clean the tile.

2 Prepare the mortar (page 99) from a bag of dry mixed material or make your own from one part cement to four parts sharp sand. To improve adhesion, add some PVA adhesive to the water, following the manufacturer's instructions. Do not make the mortar too wet; a firmer mix is easier to work with. Mix enough to half-fill a bucket.

3 Brush all dust away from the area round the repair.

4 Use the paintbrush and water to wet the roof and the existing mortar round the repair. This is especially necessary on a hot day when the mortar would lose its moisture too quickly and crack.

5 Brush PVA adhesive liberally all round the area of the repair to ensure good adhesion between the roof tiles at the ridge or hip and the ridge or hip tile itself.

6 Use the trowel to spread mortar on the roof on both sides of the ridge or hip. Cover the areas where the bottom edges of the tile to be fixed will lie.

Do not use too much mortar; there must be a gap under the ridge or hip tiles so that air can circulate to keep the timber below dry. If you lay too much mortar on the tiles, it could squeeze into the gap and fill it in when you are setting the ridge or hip tile into place.

7 The butt joints where two of the ridge or hip tiles meet can either be pointed with mortar or given a solid bedding of mortar. It is probably best to follow the method already used on the roof.

If you make a solid bedding, place a piece of slate or tile across the gap between the two sides of the ridge or hip to prevent mortar falling through.

8 Ridge or hip tiles must be dipped in water before they are set in place. Do this before you go up on the roof. Settle the tile on the mortar carefully so that it makes a smooth line with the neighbouring tiles.

Alternatively If the roof tiles have a curved profile, fill the gap between the down-curve and the ridge or hip tiles with pieces of tile or slate embedded in mortar.

Specially designed 'dentil slips' can be bought for this purpose.

9 Smooth the mortar between tiles and along the bottom edges. There must be no hollows in the mortar between the tiles because they could retain small pockets of rainwater.

10 If the re-fixed tile is at an end of the roof ridge, seal the open end with thin slips of tile or slate bedded in mortar. Smooth the end so that rainwater will flow off readily.

11 If you have been replacing the lowest tile on the hip, make sure the protecting hip iron has not been dislodged; remake its fixings if necessary. Then fill the end of the tile with mortar.

Repairs to verges

A roof with only two main slopes is usually sealed with mortar where the slopes meet the gable ends of the house – the verges.

Before you start You can seal any minor cracks in the mortar with roof-and-gutter sealant injected with an applicator gun.

If you choose a sealant to match the mortar, the repair will not be noticeable. For larger cracks you will have to make the repair with mortar.

Tools *Ladder with a stand-off bracket; cold chisel; club hammer; brush; paintbrush; small trowel.*

Materials *Dry mortar mix, or cement and sharp sand; PVA adhesive; bucket of water. Perhaps narrow slips of tile.*

1 With the chisel and hammer, chip away all cracked and crumbling mortar, leaving only sound mortar in place.

2 Prepare the mortar (page 99) from a bag of dry mixed material or from one part cement to four parts sharp sand. To improve adhesion, add PVA adhesive to the water, following the manufacturer's instructions. Avoid making the mixture too wet. Make enough to half-fill a bucket.

3 Brush all dust away, then dampen the area with some water using a paintbrush before brushing on PVA adhesive.

4 Use the trowel to press the mortar firmly into the areas that have been prepared. Knock it in with the side of the trowel to make sure that there are no pockets of air.

5 Smooth the surface of the mortar and clean away any excess. Do not leave any ledges or hollows in the mortar that could retain rainwater.

Repairs to metal valleys

Where two roof slopes meet at the bottom, the long narrow gap between them is sealed by a tray of aluminium alloy, lead or zinc. This metal valley is overlapped by the tiles or slates, which drain rainwater into it to be carried into the gutters at the eaves.

Valleys must be kept waterproof and clear of obstructions. If moss, leaves or other debris accumulates, rainwater will build up at the obstruction and spill over the edges of the valley onto the timbers and into the roof space.

If a metal valley has developed a fine crack or is showing the first signs of corrosion, it can be repaired with a liquid bitumen compound. Liquid bitumen can also be used to make a temporary repair if the valley needs replacing.

Holes or splits in a metal valley can be covered with a self-adhesive metal-backed flashing strip. If slight corrosion has set in over a large area, flashing strip can be used to cover the entire valley.

Repairing with liquid bitumen

Stir the waterproofing compound before you apply it. You can use it on a damp, but not wet, surface. Do not use it, however, if rain or frost are expected within about 24 hours.

Tools *Ladder with a stand-off bracket; roof ladder; wire brush; a spreader for the roof-and-gutter sealant; sharp knife or scissors; soft brush or broom.*

Materials *Roof-and-gutter sealant; roofing felt or cooking foil; liquid bitumen waterproofing compound; bucket of water.*

1 Use the wire brush to clean away dirt and loose metal fragments from the area of the valley that is going to be repaired.

2 Spread roof-and-gutter sealant over the damaged area and at least 50mm beyond it.

3 Cut out a piece of roofing felt or cooking foil to cover the damage and extend at least 50mm beyond it. Press the felt or foil down over the sealant.

4 Spread another layer of sealant on top of the felt or foil.

5 Brush the liquid bitumen waterproofing compound over the repair. As a precaution against leaks, you can brush it over the whole valley. Apply it with a soft brush or broom, dipping the brush in water and shaking it each time before you load it with the waterproofer. Brush the compound on with even strokes, working in the same direction all the time.

Making repairs with flashing strip

Tools *Ladder with a stand-off bracket; roof ladder; wire brush; damp cloth; paintbrush; sharp knife or strong scissors; old wallpaper seam roller.*

Materials *Medium-coarse abrasive paper; flashing-strip primer; self-adhesive metal-backed flashing strip.*

1 Use the wire brush to clean away loose fragments from round the crack or hole.

2 Rub over the area with abrasive paper.

3 Wipe the surface clean with the damp cloth and allow it to dry completely.

4 Apply a coat of flashing-strip primer to the area of the repair, extending it at least 50mm beyond the damage. Leave it to dry for the time recommended by the manufacturer – usually about 30 minutes.

5 Cut out a piece of flashing strip to extend at least 50mm beyond the crack or hole all round. Cut it with a knife or pair of scissors, then peel off the backing.

6 Press the flashing strip firmly into position, using the wallpaper seam roller to bed it down smoothly.

Repairs to flashings

Where a tile or slate roof meets a wall, there is a flashing to seal the join – for example at the meeting of a roof with a chimney stack and the meeting of a bay window or porch roof with the house wall.

Flashings fitted when the house is built are usually strips of lead which can deteriorate with age. Depending on the extent of the deterioration, it may not be necessary to replace the flashing. Small repairs are quite easily achieved.

Fine cracks To repair a fine crack, inject some bituminous sealant or other roof-and-gutter sealant into it with an applicator gun and cartridge. Some sealants are available in different colours so you can choose one that will make the repair less noticeable.

Small holes or slight corrosion A patch of self-adhesive flashing strip will make a sound repair over a small hole or where there are the first signs of corrosion.

Use the method described for a roof valley under Making repairs with flashing strip (opposite).

Renewing flashing mortar The top edge of a flashing is sandwiched into the mortar between two courses of bricks. Sometimes it works loose and lets in water.

Repoint the joint (page 44), but first push the edge of the flashing back into the gap between courses of bricks.

If the flashing springs out, wedge it with blocks of wood until the pointing has hardened. Then withdraw the blocks and fill the holes with mortar.

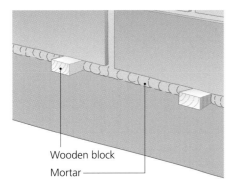

Wooden block
Mortar

Replacing a flashing

If a flashing is badly cracked or corroded, replace it with a self-adhesive metal-backed flashing strip. Unlike lead flashing, adhesive flashing is not tucked into the mortar joints.

Tools *Ladder with a stand-off bracket; roof ladder; plugging chisel and club hammer; pointing trowel; wire brush; paintbrush; sharp craft knife; old wallpaper seam roller.*

Materials *Mortar for repointing (page 99); flashing-strip primer; self-adhesive metal-backed flashing-strip.*

1 Chip out any mortar that is still holding the flashing in the joints between bricks or masonry. Use the plugging chisel and hammer. Protect your hands and eyes.

2 Strip away the old flashing.

3 Use the wire brush to clean away loose mortar and dirt from the area to be repaired.

4 Repoint the joints between the courses of bricks or masonry (page 44). Let the new pointing dry out overnight.

5 Paint a coat of flashing primer on the wall (or chimney) and roof where the strip is to go. Let it dry for 30 minutes to an hour, according to the manufacturer's instructions.

6 Cut two lengths of flashing strip, each the full length of the area to be sealed.

7 Peel off the backing of the first strip and put the strip in position, letting the width lie equally on the roof and the wall (or chimney stack). Roll the strip with the wallpaper seam roller to smooth it out and ensure that it is well stuck.

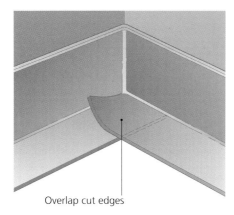

Overlap cut edges

8 At internal corners, make a snip in the lower edge of the strip and overlap the cut edges.

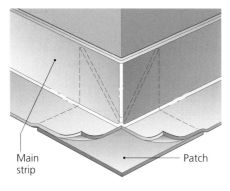

Main strip — Patch

9 At external corners, fit a square patch before the main strip; make a cut from one corner of the patch to the middle. Set the patch with the centre at the point where the wall angle meets the roof and the cut running upwards. Let the cut edges splay out round the angle. In the main strip make a cut in the bottom edge and let the cut edges splay apart over the patch. Trim off any excess at the points.

10 Peel the backing off the second strip and apply it so that its top edge is 50mm above the top edge of the first layer. Treat any corners as in the first strip. Again smooth the strip out and bed it down well with the wallpaper seam roller.

Minor repairs to flat roofs

Small blisters or cracks are the most common minor defects in felt-covered flat roofs.

Before you start Scrape off any chippings carefully with an old wallpaper scraper. You can repair small blisters or cracks with a roof-and-gutter sealant (below), with self-adhesive flashing strip (see Making a temporary repair to a cracked tile or slate, page 23), or with brush-on liquid rubber (right). Repair damaged flashings as described on page 31.

Curing bubbles A bubble may form in the felt where moisture has seeped under it and swollen in the heat of the sun. Cut a cross in the blister with a sharp knife and fold back the four flaps of felt.

Let them dry, then stick them down with a cold felt adhesive before patching the damaged area with a piece of self-adhesive flashing strip or a bitumen mastic repair compound.

Replace any roof chippings when the repairs are complete.

Bituminous sealant Apply sealant from an applicator gun to mend small cracks in roofing felt and roof tiles.

Repairing a cracked flashing

Changes in temperature and normal house movement put the flashings under stress and may cause cracks where water can seep in. The resulting wet patch indoors, however, can be several feet away from the crack because the water may run along the roof beams before dripping onto the ceiling. The crack may be difficult to spot. When you have located it, repair it with self-adhesive flashing strip (see Making repairs with flashing strip, page 30).

Repairing a hole or crack with liquid rubber

If cracks develop on a flat roof that is covered with felt or asphalt, treat the whole area with brush-on liquid rubber.

Calculate the area of the roof in square metres and buy the amount of liquid rubber recommended by the manufacturer. Liquid rubber is sold in containers ranging from 1kg to 20kg.

Tools *Ladder; stiff brush and shovel; an old 100mm paintbrush or a small broom for the liquid rubber. Perhaps a paintbrush for primer.*

Materials *Liquid rubber. Perhaps primer for liquid rubber.*

1 Use the stiff brush and shovel to clear the area of loose chippings and dirt.

2 If the area has previously been treated with a tar-bitumen coating – which gives a black, slightly rough covering – brush on a coat of primer for liquid rubber. Leave it to dry overnight.

3 Brush on a coat of liquid rubber, using all the recommended amount for the area. Leave it to dry thoroughly for 48 hours. After an hour it will be sufficiently dry not to be affected by rain.

4 Brush on a second coat of rubber, using the same amount as before.

A replacement flashing

If the flashing has cracked or corroded so much that an adhesive patch may not be able to make firm contact all over the damaged area, strip away all the flashing and plan to replace it with self-adhesive flashing strip as described in Replacing a flashing (page 31).

Seal the joint between roof and parapet (or house wall) with roof-and-gutter sealant before you apply the primer.

If your parapet is only one course of brickwork or masonry high, let the second layer of flashing overlap onto the top.

Mending a corrugated plastic roof

A corrugated plastic roof is ideal where extra light is required, but it can become brittle and need repairing.

Before you start Measure the profile of the existing plastic on the roof before you go to buy new sheeting. The sheets may have a round or a box profile and the difference between the lowest and highest points of the profile can vary from 38 to 150mm.

If the new plastic does not exactly match the old in profile, it will not make snug overlaps. The length of the screws you use must be the difference between the low and high points of the profile plus at least 25mm to penetrate the wood.

To reduce the cost of the repair, you can fit a patch. However, the patch will have to be the width of a full sheet and extend over a roof timber at top and bottom to be screwed in place.

Temporary repairs to a corrugated plastic roof can be made using clear waterproof tape. Ensure surfaces are clean and dry before pressing the tape into place.

Tools *Sharp knife; tack lifter; screwdriver; fine-toothed saw; hand drill with blunt twist bit, or electric soldering iron with 5mm bit; steel measuring tape.*

Materials *Enough corrugated plastic sheeting to make the repair with adequate overlaps; No. 8 galvanised screws of appropriate length; protective screw caps; transparent waterproof glazing tape.*

Fitting a patch

1 Use a felt pen to mark cutting lines on the damaged panel showing the area for removal. Make the top line just below a timber support and the bottom line just above a timber support.

2 Prise off the screw caps with the tack lifter and take out all the screws that were securing the panel. Carefully remove the whole panel.

3 Cut the patch to overlap the guidelines on the old panel by 75mm at top and bottom. Then cut along the guidelines on the old panel to remove the damaged part. Hold the saw at a shallow angle and support the sheet on both sides of the cut. If you have to cut to the sheet to width, cut along the valleys of the sheeting.

4 Lay the plastic for the bottom of the slope in place first. Make screw holes through the peaks that are over timbers. Make the holes at intervals of about 450mm across the panel immediately above the cross timbers. You can melt the holes with a fine soldering iron or start them with a bradawl. Drive in the screws across the bottom edge. Do not overtighten.

5 Lay the next piece of plastic up the slope; let its bottom edge overlap 75mm onto the piece below.

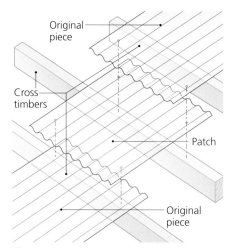

Original piece

Cross timbers

Patch

Original piece

6 Drill screw holes through peaks on the overlap at 450mm intervals. Drive screws through into the timbers but do not overtighten them.

7 Lay the top piece of plastic sheet in place overlapping the previous piece by 75mm.

8 Drill and screw the bottom edge as for the previous piece.

9 Drill holes if necessary at the top edge and screw it in place.

10 Push caps on all the screws.

11 Fit new flashing strip (page 30) where the plastic sheet meets the wall. Press it down well into the valleys.

12 Seal the edges where the layers of plastic sheeting overlap at the sides with strips of the glazing tape.

Fitting a whole panel

1 Cut away any flashing at the top of the damaged panel.

2 Prise off the screw caps with the tack lifter and take out all the screws that were securing the panel, then remove the panel.

3 Cut the new panel if necessary to match the length of the old one. Keep the saw at a shallow angle and take care to support the sheet on both sides of the cut. If you have to cut to the sheet to width, cut along valleys.

4 Place the new panel in position on the roof, overlapping onto the old ones at either side. If there is another panel above or below the new one, make sure that the bottom edge of the panel higher up the slope laps onto the panel below.

5 Make screw holes across the bottom if necessary. Make the holes at intervals of about 450mm across the panel immediately above the cross timbers. Melt the holes with a fine soldering iron, start them with a bradawl, or use a blunt bit in a drill.

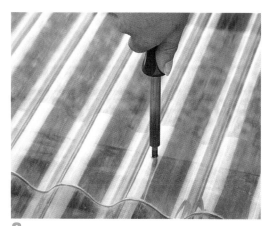

6 Drive in the screws; do not over tighten them or the plastic may split.

7 When the screws are fixed, push on screw caps. They will click into place.

8 Fit a new flashing strip (page 30) and press it down well into the valleys.

9 Seal the edges where the layers overlap with transparent waterproof glazing tape.

Re-aligning a gutter

If water forms a pool, even in a cleaned gutter, instead of running away to the downpipe, the fixing screw holding the support bracket or the gutter itself at that point may be loose.

Remove the screw, tap a wall plug into the screw hole and re-screw the bracket or gutter with a new zinc-plated screw. If, when you check, you find that no screws are loose, or conversely that several are loose, the fall of the gutter may need correcting. You may have to remove a section of gutter to reach the screws.

Tools *Ladder with a stand-off bracket; hammer; screwdriver; drill with wood bit or high-speed-steel bit, or both; spirit level.*

Materials *Wall plugs; zinc-plated No. 8 or No. 10 screws; two or more 150mm nails; string and nails.*

4 If the gutter is on brackets, as most gutters are, unscrew those that are letting the gutter sag and move them left or right slightly to new positions so that you can screw into solid wood; make sure the new screw positions align with the string line to give the correct fall.

Alternatively If the gutter is screwed direct to the fascia, raise it to align correctly with the string line and drill new holes through the gutter and into the fascia, about 50mm to the side of the original holes. Refit the gutter using new zinc-plated screws.

Alternatively If the screws through the gutter have been driven into the ends of the roof rafters, not into a fascia board, fix a string line and adjust the position of the screws to bring the gutter to the correct fall. You may have to remove a tile or slate temporarily so that you can reach the screws (pages 23 and 26).

1 Drive a long, strong nail into the fascia board near each end of the loose section of gutter, immediately below it, to support it. If the loose section is longer than 2m or the gutter is iron, drive in more nails to give it sufficient support.

2 Remove the screws that hold the gutter or its supporting brackets.

3 Fix a taut string line along the length of the fascia board immediately under the guttering. Check it is horizontal with a spirit level then lower the string at the downpipe end to give it a fall towards the downpipe of 15–20mm in every 3m.

Treating rusted gutters

Treat rust as soon as you are aware of its presence. The longer it is left, the more damage will be done and the greater the size of the repair job.

Before you start Make sure you have safety goggles to protect your eyes from flying particles when removing rust. Do not rub the metal too vigorously – it does not have to shine – just remove the rust. If the inside of the gutter cannot be seen from any upstairs window, you can use up left-over gloss paint of any colour instead of buying bitumen paint.

Tools *Ladder with a stand-off bracket; safety goggles; strong work gloves; wire brush or electric drill fitted with wire cup brush or wheel; emery cloth; paintbrush. Perhaps filling knife.*

Materials *Rust-neutralising primer; black bitumen paint or left-over gloss paint. Perhaps roof-and-gutter sealant or glass-fibre filler.*

1 Rub off smaller rust spots with the emery cloth.

2 Remove larger patches of rust with the wire brush or brush wheel fitted in the drill.

3 Apply a coat of rust-neutralising primer to the cleaned parts; and to the rest of the inside of the gutter as well, if you wish.

4 Seal any small cracks in the gutter with roof-and-gutter sealant.

5 If there is a larger crack or hole, fill it with a glass-fibre filler of the kind used for car body repairs. Be sure to smooth the filling thoroughly so there is no roughness to hold water or silt.

6 Apply a coat of black bitumen or gloss paint. Allow it to dry and apply a second.

Cleaning an overflowing gutter

Gutters should be cleaned out and checked for damage each year. The job is best done in late autumn after all the leaves have fallen.

Before you start Wear sturdy work gloves to avoid scraping your hands on rough or rusty edges or on tiles or slates.

Tools *Ladder with a stand-off bracket; protective gloves; small trowel; bucket; piece of hardboard or a large rag. Possibly a hosepipe.*

Plastic guttering parts

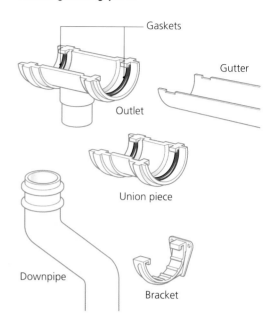

Gaskets

Gutter

Outlet

Union piece

Downpipe

Bracket

1 Put the piece of hardboard at the bottom of the downpipe to prevent debris from getting into the gully or the drain, where it could cause a blockage.

Alternatively If the downpipe goes direct into the ground, stuff the rag in the top of it.

2 Scoop out any silt, grit or other debris with the trowel and put it into the bucket. Take care not to let anything drop into the downpipe. Take care not to let any debris fall down the walls because it may cause stains that are hard to remove.

3 Unblock the downpipe and pour three or four buckets of water slowly into the gutter at the end farthest from the pipe.

Alternatively Use a hosepipe to lead water there. The water should flow quickly and smoothly to the downpipe, leaving the gutter empty.
• If a pool of water remains, the gutter needs realigning (see page 35).
• If the water leaks through cracks or bad joints, repair the gutter (facing page).
• If the water starts to overflow at the downpipe, the pipe needs cleaning out (page 39).

Repairing leaking gutter joints

Sometimes you can spot a dripping gutter from indoors, but occasionally walk round the house during heavy rain to check on all your gutters.

Rainwater dripping through gutters and splashing the house walls will cause a water stain on the outside wall and, after a time, moss and algae will grow, disfiguring the wall. If the leak is not cured, damp will penetrate the walls, causing damage indoors. Damp quickly ruins decorations and eventually causes rot in timbers.

Leaking metal gutters

A metal gutter is difficult to take apart if the nuts and bolts have corroded, so try to seal the leak by injecting roof-and-gutter sealant into the joint with an applicator gun. First scrape the joint clean and dry it with a hot-air gun. If the leak persists, you will have to dismantle and reseal the joint. Wear strong gloves to protect your hands from rough metal.

Tools *Ladder with a stand-off bracket; gloves; safety goggles; spanner; hammer; wire brush; old chisel; small trowel; paintbrush; narrow-bladed filing knife. Perhaps a junior hacksaw and nail punch.*

Materials *Metal primer; roof-and-gutter sealant; nut and bolt of correct size.*

1 Undo the nut securing the bolt in the joint piece.

Alternatively If the nut will not move, cut through the bolt with a hacksaw and take out the shank with nail punch and hammer.

2 Gently hammer the joint piece to separate it from the gutter sections.

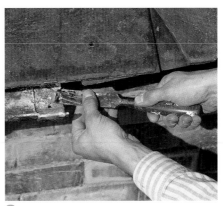

3 With the joint dismantled, chisel away the putty and clean rust from the whole joint area with the wire brush. Scoop away the debris with the trowel.

4 Apply a coat of metal primer to the gutter ends and the joint piece and leave it to dry.

5 Spread roof-and-gutter sealant onto the joint piece and reposition the gutter sections on it.

6 Secure the joint with the new nut and bolt.

Leaking plastic gutters

Where pieces of gutter join, or connect with a downpipe, they are clipped to a connector or union piece which has gaskets in it to make the union watertight.

Leakages caused by dirt forcing the seal slightly apart can be cured by cleaning. Squeeze the sides of the gutter inwards to release it from the union piece. If there is no dirt, the gaskets may need renewing.

Tools *Ladder with a stand-off bracket; filling knife.*

Materials *New gaskets or roof-and-gutter sealant.*

1 Squeeze the sides of the gutter sections in order to release them from the clips of the union piece.

2 Gently raise the end of each section of gutter in turn until you can see the gasket in the union piece. Peel the gasket away.

3 Fit the new gaskets, pressing them well into place.

Alternatively Fill the grooves for the gaskets with sealant.

4 Gently squeeze each gutter section in at sides to ease it back into the union piece clips.

Securing loose downpipes

A downpipe is held to the wall by retaining clips which are screwed into the mortar joints at intervals of about a metre.

If the pipe is not firmly held, it vibrates in strong winds, and this can loosen its joints. The sections of downpipe slot loosely one into another; do not seal them together.

Cast-iron pipes

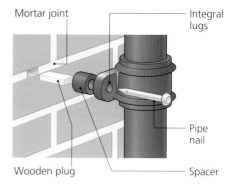

Mortar joint — Integral lugs — Pipe nail — Wooden plug — Spacer

The lugs that hold cast-iron pipes are an integral part of the pipe and are fixed with large nails called pipe nails to wooden plugs inserted in the mortar joints. If only the nails are loose, take them out and fill the hole with wood filler or insert a wall plug into it. Drive the pipe nails back in, or drive in 38mm No. 10 galvanised screws instead.

If the wooden plugs in the wall have come loose or rotted; you will have to remove them and fix new ones.

Tools *Ladder with stand-off bracket; pliers; saw; hammer. Perhaps a screwdriver.*

Materials *Softwood plugs slightly larger than the old ones; wood preservative.*

1 Pull out the old pipe nails with pliers. You can use the nails again if they come out undamaged.

2 Remove the spacers that hold the downpipe away from the wall and keep them on one side.

3 Remove one or more sections of pipe to give access to the plugs. Sections are slotted together. Raise one as high as it will go on the section above to free the lower end from the section below.

4 Take out and discard the plugs.

5 Cut new plugs, sawing and planing or chiselling them until they almost fit the holes. Treat plugs with wood preservative and tap them into place with a hammer.

6 Put back the piece or pieces of downpipe that you have removed.

7 Set the spacers in position behind each pair of lugs and drive the pipe nails through the holes to hold the downpipe securely.

Plastic downpipes

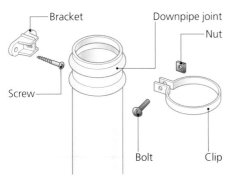

Bracket

Downpipe joint

Nut

Screw

Bolt

Clip

If a plastic downpipe comes loose from the wall, check the screws and the plastic or fibre wall plugs to see if they need renewing to give a better fixing. Use 38mm No. 10 galvanised screws.

It might be easier to move the clip up or down a little to a different mortar joint, and drill and plug new holes to get a firm fixing. Repair the old holes with mortar or exterior filler. Match the colour of the rest of the mortar to make the repair discreet.

Do not move a clip fixed at a joint in the downpipe system because it strengthens the joint. You could exchange a one-piece clip for a two-piece clip, or vice-versa, to give different fixing positions for screws.

COLLECTING RAINWATER

Position water butts beneath downpipes from the gutters on your house, outbuildings and greenhouse to collect the run-off of rainwater from your roofs for use in the garden in times of drought. Easy-to-install DIY water butts and pipes connect to the guttering system. Alternatively, complete ready-made systems are available which can be plumbed in immediately.

Water butts should be covered to prevent the growth of algae. They should also have an overflow pipe at the top, feeding into the mains drainage system or soak-away, otherwise you will have to drain off water from time to time.

If space permits, you can link a few butts together to ensure you waste as little rainfall as possible.

Unblocking a downpipe

Overflow from a gutter may be caused by a blocked downpipe.

Before you start Check what is causing the blockage. It could be a ball, a bird's nest or some other object that you can simply lift out. But the most likely obstruction is a collection of wind-blown leaves lodged in the mouth of the downpipe.

A pipe with a swan-necked section at the top is more likely to become blocked than a straight downpipe.

Another indication of a blocked down-pipe is water seeping out during heavy rain from a joint where sections of downpipe connect. Because the joints are loose, not sealed, you can tell straight away where the blockage is; it is in the section immediately below the leaking joint.

Obstructions near the top

If the downpipe is blocked near the top, you can usually clear it by probing with a length of wire. Cover the drain at the bottom of the pipe to prevent any debris from falling into it. Hook out debris if you can; if you cannot, probe until it becomes loose. Flush away remaining loose debris by pouring buckets of water down the pipe or playing a strong jet of water down it from a hose. If the pipe is straight, not swan-necked, tie rags firmly to the end of a stick (such as a bamboo garden cane) to form a ball and push the obstruction loose with it.

Obstructions out of reach

Hire a flexible drain rod to clear an obstruction lower down a pipe or in a swan-necked pipe. Or, as a last resort, dismantle the lower part of the downpipe.

Tools *Ladder with a stand-off bracket; screwdriver or pliers or box spanner; long stick. Perhaps a cold chisel and claw hammer.*

1 On a plastic downpipe, remove the screws that hold the pipe clips to the wall. Work from the bottom and remove the screws and clips up to the point it leaks. If the pipe is held by two-part brackets, undo

the bolts holding the rings to the back plates; leave the back plates in place. If the pipe is cast-iron, use pliers to pull out the large pipe nails that hold the lugs to the wall. If they are rusted, use a cold chisel and claw hammer to prise the lugs from the wall; keep the nails for re-use.

2 As you free the clips or lugs that hold it, free each section of pipe from the section below and lift it away from the wall.

3 Use a long stick to push out any obstructions inside the sections.

Alternatively Run a garden hose up the pipe to shift any blockage inside.

4 Replace the pipe section by section, working from the top down, and screw or bolt back in place the clips (or nail the lugs) that hold the section to the wall.

Preventing blockages

Wire or plastic covers are sold in different sizes for fitting in mouths of downpipes.
• If there is a hopper at the top of the downpipe, fit fine-mesh wire netting over the top, securing it with fine galvanised wire.
• If there are large deciduous trees nearby, it is worth covering gutters. Lay a strip of plastic netting over a gutter to overlap the top by about 50mm at each side. About every 1m along it, thread a length of twine through the overlaps from the underside of the gutter and tie it firmly to hold the mesh taut. Check the netting surface regularly during autumn; if leaves coat it, rain cannot enter the gutter and will spill over it.

Cleaning and maintaining gullies

A gully is an underground U-trap that prevents bulky waste from flowing into the drains. It is prone to blockage.

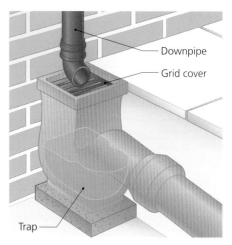

Downpipe

Grid cover

Trap

A gully is fitted at the point where a downpipe or waste pipe discharges at ground level, and is then connected to the underground drains. A yard gully is similar, but is sited away from the house and collects surface water via an open grating. The trap in the gully is there to collect solid waste material, preventing it from entering the drains and causing a blockage that would be difficult to remove.

In older properties, the water discharges into a gully above a grid fitted over the trap. This grid can become blocked with leaves and other debris, resulting in waste water splashing over the surrounding area instead of passing into the trap.

In newer properties, waste pipes discharge into soil stacks, and downpipes discharge into back-inlet gullies. Here the downpipe passes directly through the grating and into the trap, so avoiding over-flow problems. If the gully does not have to act as a yard gully, a screw-down cover provides access to the trap.

Channel gullies taking waste water via a half-round channel are especially prone to grid blockages. Prevent these by putting a cover on the gully. Cut it from outdoor-grade plywood 13–19mm thick. Make a hole for the waste pipe to pass through.

Clearing a blockage

1 Clear all debris from the gully grating. If necessary, prise out the grating and scrub it in hot soapy water.

2 If the blockage is deeper, remove the grating. Wear long rubber gloves or put your arm in a plastic bag. Reach into the trap, which may be up to 600mm deep, and scoop out as much debris as you can.

3 If the obstruction is too solid to scoop out, break it down with a garden trowel.

4 When the gully is cleared, scrub the sides with a nylon pot scourer and hose them down with a fierce jet of water. Disinfect all gloves and tools afterwards.

5 If you cannot find an obstruction in the gully, the blockage may be farther down the drain; see Clearing blocked drains, page 42.

Repairing a channel gully

A channel sometimes runs parallel with the house wall to lead water into a gully entrance or to hold water that comes too fast for the gully to take. The channel can crack or become loose. The rendering around it can also crack or develop hollows where water lodges and stagnates.

Repair damaged rendering with a mix of one part cement to four parts soft sand, with PVA building adhesive added for a better bond. Alternatively, buy a small bag of dry-mix sand-cement mortar to use instead, but add PVA adhesive to improve adhesion. Give the repair a smooth finish so that water does not collect.

Renewing a damaged gully

You will have to chip out the old one and the surrounding brick and rendering. You can buy ready-made vitrified clay channels from builders' merchants. Use the same mortar mix as for rendering repairs.

Tools *Chalk; cold chisel; club hammer; offcut of hardboard or thick card; trowel.*

Materials *Bricks; length of channel; mortar.*

1 To cut the channel to length, first measure and mark the length at several points round the pipe and join the marks with a chalk line. Lay the channel on a heap of sand and use the chisel and hammer to chip round the marked line until the channel breaks along it. Alternatively, use an angle grinder if you have one to cut the channel. Wear goggles to protect your eyes from flying dust and chippings.

2 Put a piece of hardboard over the gully inlet to prevent debris from getting in.

3 Chip out the damaged channel and the mortar and any bricks round it. If the bricks round the gully entrance are damaged, chip these out as well. Brush up the debris.

4 Mix the mortar and spread a thick layer where the channel will lie. Bed down the channel on it, setting it so that it slopes slightly towards the gully.

5 Lay a course of bricks (page 103) on edge to make a low retaining wall round the channel and gully. Set them on a bed of mortar and leave a gap of at least 25mm between the channel and the bricks alongside it. Nearer the gully the gap may need to be wider.

6 Fill the gap between the channel and the bricks with mortar.

7 Slope the mortar smoothly up to the brick surround and make sure there are no hollows to trap water.

Clearing blocked drains

Below ground, pipes carry water and waste from the house to the main drain outside the boundary of the property, or to a cesspool or septic tank. Rainwater may be led separately into the drain or into a soakaway.

Tools *Drain rods fitted with a 100mm diameter rubber plunger; pair of long rubber gloves; strong garden spade; hose; disinfectant; watering can.*

Before you start Remember that the pipes below ground are laid in straight lines for as much of their route as possible. Where a change of direction is needed, the bend should be less than a right angle and there should be an inspection chamber there. A manhole cover identifies the chambers. An older property may have an interceptor chamber near the boundary before the house drain joins the main drain (see right).

The first sign of a blocked drain may be the failure of WCs and baths to drain quickly and efficiently, or an overflowing inspection chamber or gully. A gully may be cleared by cleaning (see page 40). Otherwise you will have to clear the drain with rods. You can hire rods and various heads. Wear rubber gloves for the work.

1 Locate the blockage. You will have to lift the manhole covers; a strong garden spade will raise the edge enough for you to grasp the cover. Inspect the chamber that is nearer to the main drain, septic tank or cesspool than the overflowing chamber or gully. If it is empty, the blockage is in the drain between this chamber and the higher one or the gully. If the chamber is full, inspect the chamber next nearest to the main drain or septic tank. If the chamber nearest the main drain is full, the blockage is between it and the main drain. If the drain leads to a septic tank and the last chamber is full, have the tank emptied.

Interceptor chambers If you have to clear a blockage between an interceptor chamber on your property and the main drain, you will have to insert the rods through the rodding eye. At this chamber, the drain drops through a U-trap similar to the one in a gully. The trap is there to prevent waste from the main drain entering your house drains, but it also prevents you from pushing rods through. Above the mouth of the trap there is a short projection of pipe with a plug in it. When you locate and pull out the plug,

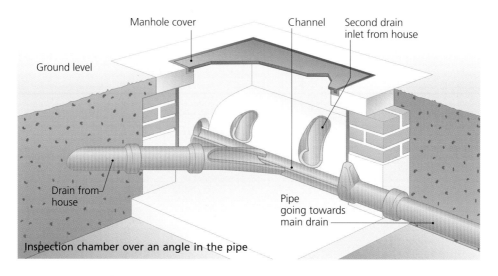

Manhole cover   Channel   Second drain inlet from house

Ground level

Drain from house

Pipe going towards main drain

Inspection chamber over an angle in the pipe

2 To clear the blockage in a main drain system, insert the rod fitted with the plunger into a chamber at one end of the blocked section; it does not matter which of the two. If it is the empty chamber, you can see where the mouth of the pipe is, but if you work from the full chamber, you will have to probe with the plunger until you find the mouth.

3 Add more rods as necessary to work the plunger along the pipe to the blockage. Always turn the rods clockwise as you work; if you turn them counter-clockwise,

they may unscrew and be left in the drain to cause a greater problem. Keep pushing against the obstruction and then withdrawing the plunger a little way. If this will not shift the blockage, withdraw the rods and exchange the plunger for a corkscrew attachment, which will break up a tightly packed obstruction.

4 Complete the clearance by directing a strong jet of water down the drain from a hosepipe, or by filling the bath and sink and releasing the water in one gush.

5 Hose down the rods and gloves thoroughly and drench them with diluted disinfectant poured from a watering can.

Testing drains

If the drains are not blocked, but a persistent foul smell or unexpectedly wet ground make you suspect that there is a leak somewhere, arrange for the environmental health department to test the drains. You can get in touch with the department at your local authority offices.

you can insert the drain rods through the hole, or rodding eye. The trap, however, may still be blocked and you will have to scoop out the blockage with an old garden trowel bent to a right angle. When the chamber and trap are clear, hose them down thoroughly to make sure waste can flow out easily. You can either replace the plug or you can mortar a piece of tile over the eye. If you need to open the rodding eye again, the tile will knock off easily with a crowbar and hammer.

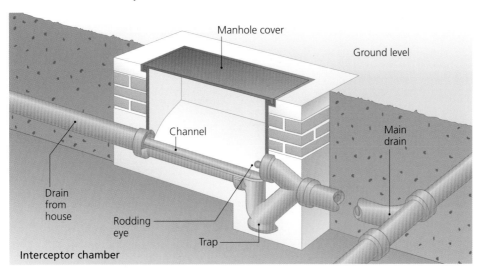

Manhole cover

Ground level

Channel

Main drain

Drain from house

Rodding eye

Trap

Interceptor chamber

Minor repairs to walls

Cracks, deteriorating mortar, damp and damaged brickwork are all easily repaired when the problem is small.

Repointing a wall

Where mortar joints in a wall are cracked or crumbling, use a raking out tool or a club hammer and plugging chisel to take out the old mortar to a depth of about 15mm, ready for repointing.

Before you start One problem when you are patching a number of joints, is to match the colour of the mortar with that of the surrounding joints. The only way to do this is to experiment with a few different mortar mixes (page 99), using varying amounts of sand and lime. Take a note of each mix and repoint a few joints at a time. Wait a week or two for the mortar to dry thoroughly and show its final colour before you decide on the best mix to complete the job.

Carry out repointing as in Pointing the joints (page 105), matching the shape with the surrounding joints. Before you apply new mortar, clean any dust from the joints then brush water into them. If you do not wet them, the joints will soak up moisture from the mortar and it will dry out too fast.

Dealing with a crack

Mortar is meant to be weaker than bricks or masonry so that it offers less resistance if movement beneath the foundations causes any strain on the wall. The mortar will crack before the bricks or masonry. A single crack confined to a mortar joint, even through several courses, usually indicates limited amount of soil settlement. A repair can be made by repointing.

A brick may be cracked by minor settlement. You can replace it yourself. If a crack runs through more than the odd brick, there is a more serious strain on the foundations. Get a professional builder to deal with it as soon as possible.

Replacing a damaged brick

Remove a damaged brick by chipping away the surrounding mortar with a club hammer and cold chisel.

You can speed up the process by drilling a series of holes into the mortar first. Drill to a depth of about 100mm, then cut into the mortar all round to release the damaged brick. Chop as much mortar out of the resulting cavity as you can, ready for the new brick to be fitted. Dampen the cavity very well. Spread mortar on the base of the cavity and on the top and sides of the new brick. Tap the brick into the cavity with the trowel handle. When it is properly seated, trim away the excess mortar. Point the joints to match the others on the wall.

Dealing with efflorescence

The white powdery deposit called efflorescence is caused by dampness, which draws chemical salts from the bricks or mortar to the surface. It is harmless, and will disappear from a newly built wall once it has dried out.

You can discourage efflorescence by coating a wall with a silicone-based water repellent (right). If efflorescence does form, brush it off or treat it with a chemical masonry cleaner available from a builders' merchant. Do not wash off efflorescence; the damp aggravates the problem.

Keeping out damp with silicone water repellent

Silicone water repellent will normally cure damp problems on external walls. It stops rain from getting into the brick but it lets the wall 'breathe' so that moisture already in the material can evaporate.

If damp patches persist, you should get professional advice.

Tools *Bucket of water; wire brush; a clean old paintbrush, 100–150mm wide; paint kettle. Perhaps a ladder.*

Materials *Silicone water repellent such as Aquaseal 66; white spirit for cleaning brush.*

1 Clean the surface with water and the wire brush. Wait until the surface has dried.

2 Tape paper over the window glass, frame and ledges. You will not be able to remove splashes of silicone from them. Cover any part of a drive or path adjoining the wall you are treating. The silicone could otherwise cause blotches.

3 Pour the repellent into the paint kettle and apply a generous amount of the liquid with an old paintbrush, so that you can see it flowing down the wall.

4 If the surface soaks up all the liquid – because it is very porous – apply a second coat before the first coat dries.

5 Use white spirit to clean the paintbrush and the paint kettle when the job is finished.

Patching large holes in a rendered wall

Before you start When large slabs of rendering fall away from the wall, it is usually because a weak rendering mix has been used and become porous, or because damp has penetrated behind the layer of rendering, perhaps through a crack.

Sometimes the rendering may appear intact, when in fact it has separated from the wall behind. Check the rendering from time to time, tapping it lightly with a hammer; undamaged areas will make dead sound while defective areas give a hollow sound or fall away.

Carry out rendering work in mild weather. Frost can freeze the water in the rendering, which may cause premature cracking.

Preparing the rendering Mix the rendering from six parts plastering sand, one part cement and one part hydrated lime. Do not use builders' sand or the rendering will crack when it dries out. Use enough water to make the mixture easy to work with – not too stiff, not too sloppy.

Mix up small batches at a time. The rendering will become too stiff to spread after about 20 minutes. It is applied in two coats – a thick undercoat called the floating coat, and a thinner finishing coat.

Tools *Bolster chisel; club hammer; brush; wet sponge or cloth; steel plastering trowel; old pointed trowel or square of wood with nails driven through to project at about 38mm intervals; straight edged length of wood longer than the width of the patch; damp sponge or clean wooden float. Perhaps a ladder and a plugging chisel.*

Materials *Ready-mixed mortar for rendering.*

1 Use the bolster chisel and hammer to cut away any loose rendering to leave a sound edge round the patch.

2 Clean out any crumbling joints in the brickwork or masonry. Clean them out to a depth of 15mm with the plugging chisel and club hammer. Brush out all debris.

3 Thoroughly wet the area to be repaired with a sponge or cloth soaked in water. This prevents rendering from losing moisture into the wall and drying too quickly, which could cause crumbling later.

4 Apply the first coat of rendering. Take some of the mixture on the steel trowel with the handle downwards. Spread it onto the wall, starting from the bottom of the patch and pressing the lower edge of the trowel hard against the wall as you sweep it smoothly upwards. Continue until the rendering is smooth and about 5mm below the level of the wall surface.

5 As the rendering begins to stiffen after about 20 minutes – scratch a criss-cross of lines in it with the old trowel or spiked wood to make a key for the top coat.

6 Leave the first coat to dry for at least 14 hours, then apply the finishing coat. Use the same rendering mixture as for the floating coat. This time, start at the top left of the patch. Sweep the trowel lightly across from left to right to spread the rendering over the area, leaving it standing slightly proud of the surface.

7 Continue applying trowel loads from top to bottom down the patch spreading them from left to right. Mix more small batches of rendering as necessary, but work quickly.

8 Just before the rendering begins to set – about 15 minutes after it has been applied – draw the straight-edged piece of wood upwards over the rendering to level it with the wall. Hold the wood horizontally and make sure that you are pressing its ends firmly against the wall on either side of the patch. If any hollows are showing after levelling off, fill them quickly with more rendering and level them with the straight-edged piece of wood. As the rendering starts to set, smooth its surface gently with damp sponge or a damp wooden float.

Repairing cracks on a rendered wall

Before you start Hairline crazing on the surface of rendering does not need filling. Cracks that go deeper than the surface do need filling to keep the wall weatherproof. Fill the cracks with exterior filler or with rendering. Filler is convenient but uneconomical for more than one or two cracks. You can buy dry-mixed rendering in small quantities or you can make your own. The repair will show until the wall is repainted; an invisible repair is impossible to achieve.

Tools *Filling knife; brush; wet sponge or cloth; old paintbrush. Perhaps a bolster chisel and club hammer and a ladder.*

Materials *PVA adhesive; mortar mix for rendering or exterior filler.*

1 Draw the edge of a filling knife through the crack to form it into a V with the point of the V at the surface of the rendering and the wider part against the wall.

You can use a bolster chisel and club hammer instead of the filling knife if you find it easier.

The shape will anchor the filler below the surface and the crack is unlikely to open again.

2 Brush out the fragments and dust from the cavity to leave it as clean as possible.

3 Wet the cavity with a sponge or cloth dipped in water.

4 Paint all the inside of the cavity with PVA adhesive to improve adhesion of the filler.

5 Press the filler or rendering into the crack with the filling knife. Prod the knife into the cavity to make sure there are no air pockets in it. Smooth the filling level with the wall surface. Redecorate the wall when the filler has dried.

Repairing pebbledash

It is simple enough to repair damaged pebbledash, but the repair will be visible unless the wall is to be painted because the new chippings and the rendering beneath will not match the original colour. You will need about 5kg of chippings to cover a square metre.

Tools *Cold chisel; club hammer; brush; wet sponge or cloth; steel trowel; sheet of polythene; small scoop; wooden float. Perhaps a ladder.*

Materials *Soft sand and cement or dry ready-mix rendering mortar; PVA building adhesive; water; chippings.*

1 Prepare the area for repair as for Patching large holes (page 45) and mix and lay on a first coat of rendering in the same way, but leave it about 15mm below the level of the wall surface.

2 Wash the chippings and drain them in a garden sieve.

3 Mix the rendering for the top coat, known as the butter coat. Use five parts of sand to one cement and add some PVA building adhesive.
  Mix it to a slightly softer consistency than the first coat to make sure that it is still soft when you apply the chippings.
  Apply the top coat; if you have a large area to repair, work on a section which you can complete within 20 minutes before the coat starts to set.

4 Spread a sheet of polythene on the ground below the repair. Throw small scoops of pebbles hard at the rendering until it is evenly covered. Gather up and re-use the chippings that fall to the ground.

Alternatively Lift batches of pebbles up to the wall on a hawk and use a float to push them off the hawk and into the wet mortar.

5 When you have pebbledashed the patched area, press the wooden float lightly all over it to bed the chippings into the surface. Continue in the same way until the repair is complete.

Making a hole in an external wall

When fitting a fan or an airbrick in a cavity wall, you will have to bridge the cavity with ducting or a sleeve liner. You may also have to cut through insulation material in the cavity.

Drill a guide hole right through the wall. You may need to hire extra-long masonry drill bits for this – a bit 260mm long for a solid wall, or 300mm long for a cavity wall.

Tools *Heavy-duty hammer-action power drill; long and standard length masonry drill bits; club hammer; sharp cold chisel and bolster chisel; pencil or chalk; work gloves; safety goggles; pointing trowel.*

Materials *Bag of dry ready-mixed bricklaying mortar. For a cavity wall: ducting or sleeve liner.*

1 Mark the outline of the hole on the inside wall at the required position.

2 Make sure there are no pipes or cables in the way. If the inner leaf of a cavity wall is timber-framed, make sure you will not cut through a stud. Adjust the position of the outline if necessary.

3 Transpose the outline to the outside wall. Drill the guide hole through the wall from inside, and mark the outside wall from where the drill tip emerges. For a circular hole, drill through the centre of the marked area. For a square or rectangular hole, drill through at each corner of the marked area. Withdraw the drill bit from time to time to cool it and remove dust.

4 Wear safety goggles to protect your eyes from flying dust and debris. Cut away the plaster at the marked area inside, using a club hammer and bolster chisel. Then switch to a cold chisel and chip away the mortar between the bricks so you can dislodge them whole if possible. Work from both sides of the wall.

5 In an uninsulated cavity wall, plug the lower section of the cavity with rags to stop debris falling into it as you cut through. If the cavity is filled with foam insulation material, cut through it with a knife.

6 When the hole is complete, fit the ducting. If it is a cavity wall, fit a liner across the wall cavity. Make good round it with mortar.

Installing an airbrick

An airbrick ventilates a room or under-floor space, and is either up near a ceiling or low down under the floorboards. Underfloor airbricks are usually sited at least 150mm above ground level, and if possible below the level of the damp-proof course.

Some airbricks are made of clay, others are made of galvanised steel or plastic. All are either one, two or three bricks deep.

The amount of air a brick lets through depends on the type of holes that it has. A single brick with a square grid has roughly 1500mm^2 of opening compared with the 5500mm^2 of a steel vent with vertical slots.

A damaged airbrick provides a way for vermin to get into the house under the floorboards. Replace it as soon as you can; do not block it temporarily as this decreases ventilation under the floor, and can lead to rot in the joists and floorboards.

HELPFUL TIP

If the hole is square, check that it coincides with as many whole bricks as possible to make their removal easier – adjust the outline to do so if necessary. If the hole is circular, position it round a whole brick that can be removed from the centre of the area. If you need to make a round hole for an extractor fan or a new soil pipe, you can make a hole up to 150mm in diameter with a hired combi-hammer and a core drill. This will cut a neat round hole ready for the fan duct or soil pipe to be fitted.

1 To fit a new airbrick for extra ventilation, make a hole of the required size through the wall. If the brick is to be sited below the floorboards, you will be able to work only from the outside.

2 To replace a damaged airbrick, remove the old one by chipping out the mortar round it with a hammer and cold chisel (see page 44).

3 Check the liner behind the airbrick in a cavity wall, and replace if in poor condition.

4 Before fitting the airbrick, dampen the edges of the hole with water. Spread mortar in the base of the hole and on the top and sides of the new airbrick.

5 Push the airbrick into place, or tap it in with the brick trowel handle. Trim off excess mortar from the joint and point it to match the surrounding mortar joints.

6 Poke a stick or a piece of wire through the openings in the new airbrick to make sure no mortar is caught inside them that might obstruct the flow of air.

7 If the hole goes into a room, make good the inside of the hole with a filler if necessary. Then fit a plastic grille over the opening, using either a contact adhesive or screws and wall plugs.

Choosing a cavity-wall liner

In a cavity wall, a liner behind the airbrick stops the airflow being lost in the cavity. Special terracotta liners are available from builders' merchants. Straight liners are used for an airbrick fitted below a damp-proof course. For an airbrick above the course, use an inclined liner, which raises the inside hole and stops rain blowing through. Fitting an inclined liner is a job for a builder.

Recognising and treating damp

Damp patches at skirting-board level on an interior wall, or a tidemark as high as a metre above floor level, are two signs of damp rising from the ground.

Damp prevention

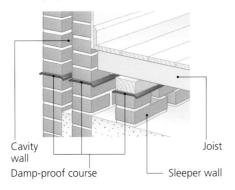

Cavity wall

Joist

Damp-proof course

Sleeper wall

To prevent damp from rising, houses are built with a damp-proof course (DPC). This is an impermeable plastic strip in modern houses, or a layer of slates or hard engineering bricks in older properties.

In most houses (except very old ones built without a DPC), you will see a thicker than usual horizontal line of pointing about 150mm above ground level, running right round the external walls. This line indicates the position of the DPC.

Defects in the damp-proofing

If the DPC deteriorates or becomes damaged, or if there is no DPC, damp is able to rise through the house walls. Rising damp will also occur if the DPC is bridged by damp material reaching above it against the outside wall – a rockery, for example, a flowerbed or even a temporary pile of building sand.

Rising damp may occur because a path or drive is too close to, or is higher than, the level of the DPC. Paths and drives must be at least 150mm below the DPC so that rainwater cannot splash above it. Where necessary, lower the path or drive surface if at all possible.

Alternatively, dig a 300mm wide channel alongside the outside wall of the house and fill it with gravel to stop rainwater splashing the wall above the DPC.

If such alterations are not practical, build a concrete skirting against the foot of the outside wall. Use a waterproofing agent in the concrete to make it impervious to water. Make the skirting reach at least 150mm higher than the path or drive and ensure there is no gap between the wall and skirting, into which water could run. Make the top of the skirting slope down from the wall so that water will run off it readily.

Repairing rot with wood-repair products

The easiest way to repair rot in a wooden window is to use a combination of wood repairing products, such as a liquid wood hardener, high-performance wood filler and wood preservative pellets.

Before you start Make sure the item you are repairing is made of painted wood – because the repair will show up on stained or varnished wood.

Tools *Old chisel, about 13mm wide; paint scraper; hot-air gun; paintbrush for applying wood hardener; filling knife; power drill; 10mm twist drill bit; hand or power sander; paintbrush for applying finishing coats to the window.*

Materials *Wood repair products (as listed above); clear wood preservative; primer, undercoat and gloss paint.*

1 Use a hot-air gun or chemical paint stripper to soften old paint, then scrape it off to reveal the extent of the rotten wood.

2 Dig away the worst of the rot with an old chisel. There is no need to cut back right into sound timber.

3 If the timber is wet it must be dried out. Saturated wood can be covered with a flap of plastic, taped along the top, so that it dries out naturally over a couple of weeks. If it is only damp, dry it rapidly with a hot-air gun. Take care to keep the air flow away from the glass, or you might crack it.

4 When the wood is thoroughly dry, flood the rotten area with brush-loads of wood hardener. The liquid penetrates the wood, and hardens it as it dries, to give a firm base for the filler. Pay particular attention to exposed end grain. Keep flooding on the hardener until it stops soaking readily into the wood and begins to stay on the surface. Let it harden overnight.

5 Mix a small amount of the high-performance wood filler according to the instructions on the container and apply it as quickly as you can to the hole. The filler will start to harden in about five minutes – even quicker in hot weather.

6 Fill in deep cavities with a succession of layers. Because the filler hardens so quickly, even deep holes can be filled in a very short time.

HELPFUL TIP

If the rot is close to a joint in the window, strengthen it with a flat steel L-shaped corner plate. Recess the corner plate to lie flush with the surface of the wood so that it is not noticeable after it is painted.

PREVENTING WET ROT

Outdoor woodwork is prone to wet rot. The wood darkens and starts to crumble as the fungus that causes the condition attacks damp wood.

The best prevention is to ensure that any new timber is treated with wood preservative (page 83), and to apply regular fresh coats of wood preservative, varnish or paint. Seal round frames with a frame sealant to prevent moisture from penetrating.

Repairing rot with new wood

The traditional way of repairing rot in a window is to cut back the rotten part to sound wood and to insert a new piece.

Before you start Wood used for the repair should match original wood in the window if it has a stained or varnished finish.

Replacing a section of sill or frame

Tools *Pencil; combination square; tenon saw or general purpose saw; chisel, about 20mm wide; mallet; vice; power drill and twist drill bits; paintbrush; plane.*

Materials *Wood to suit size of rotten section; clear wood preservative; zinc-plated No. 10 screws about 50mm long; wood dowels (same diameter as screw heads); waterproof wood adhesive; paint, varnish or preservative wood stain.*

1 Mark cutting lines on the frame about 50mm beyond signs of rot. Draw two right-angled lines on the face of the frame and then mark two more lines at about 45° to the face to form a wedge shape.

2 Using the tenon saw or general purpose saw, cut along the lines as far as possible. Brickwork may prevent you from sawing too far into a sill.

3 Complete the cut with a sharp chisel. Try to leave straight flat sides that will form a tight joint with the new wood.

4 Hold a piece of new wood against the cut-out and mark the edges of the cut-out on it with a pencil to give a cutting line.

5 Cut out the new piece with a saw and trim it with the saw or a plane until it is a good fit in the cut-out. It is better if its faces stand slightly proud of the surrounding surface.

6 Treat the cut surfaces of the frame and the new wood with clear wood preservative and allow it to dry.

7 Glue the new wood in place, holding it with G-cramps until the glue is dry.

8 Drill pilot and clearance holes for fixing screws, about 125mm apart.

7 Leave the surface of the filled hole as level as you can. After about 30 minutes it can be smoothed level with the surrounding wood with a hand or power sander. This will show up any areas where the filler is still too low.

8 Wipe away the dust and apply more filler, sanding down again afterwards so that the surface is level and smooth.

9 Drill 10mm holes about 20mm deep and 50mm apart in the wood around the repair.

10 Push one of the wood preservative pellets into each hole and then seal it with the wood filler. While the wood is dry, the pellets will remain inactive, but as soon as it becomes wet the pellets will release a fungicide which will prevent wood rot.

11 Coat any bare wood with clear wood preservative.

12 Paint the bare wood with primer and undercoat. Then give the whole window at least two coats of exterior gloss paint.

9 Drill out the holes about 15mm deep to the same diameter as the screw heads so that the heads will be sunk well below the wood surface.

10 Insert the screws and plug the holes with pieces of glued wood dowel. Drive them firmly home with the mallet.

11 Plane the faces of the insert so they are flush with the surrounding surface. Smooth with abrasive paper, and fill any gaps with exterior grade filler.

12 Finish the repair by applying paint, varnish or a preservative wood stain.

Repairing a rotten window edge

Tools *Screwdriver; panel saw; portable workbench; plane; power drill and 6mm twist drill bit; depth stop; paintbrush.*

Materials *Piece of wood to suit the size of the rotten section; clear wood preservative; waterproof wood glue; sash cramps; 6mm dowels; paint, varnish or preservative wood stain.*

1 If the rot is on the edge of an opening casement or sash, remove it so you can work on it on your workbench. A casement window is taken off by unscrewing the hinges from the frame.

To remove a sliding sash window (working from inside), prise off the staff beads from the window frame on each side. Lift the bottom sash out of the frame as far as it will go and rest it on a table or workbench. Prise out the nails holding the sash cord to the frame sides. Prise the narrow parting beads out of their grooves. Lift the top sash out and release the sash cords as before. To reassemble the window, refit the parting beads and staff beads on each side.

2 Saw off the rotten part by cutting right along the edge. Cut a replacement length of wood that is slightly oversize.

3 Treat the new wood and the cut surface of the window with clear wood preservative and allow it to dry. Ventilate the room.

4 Apply glue to the new wood and fix it in position. Hold the repair together with a pair of sash cramps until the glue has set. Wipe away any excess adhesive.

5 Reinforce the repair by drilling through the new and old wood, and driving in glued dowels. Use a 6mm twist drill bit and dowels of the same size. Before drilling, mark the correct depth of the hole on the drill bit with a depth stop, or wrap a piece of coloured adhesive tape round it.

6 When the glue has set, cut off the protruding lengths of dowel and plane the timber to the exact width and thickness of the existing wood.

7 Fill any minor gaps with exterior wood filler. Finish bare wood with paint, varnish or preservative wood stain, depending on how the rest of the window is treated.

8 Replace the repaired window in its frame.

Decorating the outside of a house

Exterior paintwork needs repainting every five years or so. Paint deteriorates at different rates, depending on how much it is exposed to wind and rain and the direct heat of the sun and how thoroughly the surface was prepared. Check the whole house from time to time for the first signs of deterioration – usually when gloss paint loses its shine, or when emulsion becomes over-powdery to the touch.

Before you start Surfaces should be clean, stable, and stripped if the paintwork is not sound. Repair damaged areas of a rendered wall and fix gutters if they are not firmly attached to the fascia board. Some weeks

Safe access is most important: your ladder or scaffold tower must be secure and in good condition. Use the components of a slot-together platform tower to make a low-level, mobile work platform.

before you intend to start painting, check that putty around windows is sound and, if not, replace it.

When to paint The best time to decorate is after a dry spell because paint will not take to a damp surface. Never paint in frosty conditions or rain, and do not paint on a very windy day – or dust and dirt will be blown onto the new paint. If it starts raining, stop painting at once and wait until the surface has completely dried out.

Before you buy the paint If you are going to change your colour scheme, make sure that the new colours will fit in with the surrounding and neighbouring buildings, especially if the house is in a terrace.

Calculate how much paint you need. Most tins indicate the average coverage of wall or other surface they will cover but rendered surfaces require more paint than smooth ones. Allow for at least two topcoats for protection against the weather. If all the walls are to be painted, estimate the total outside area of the house by multiplying the length of the walls by the height.

The easiest way to measure the height is to climb a ladder against the wall of the house, drop a ball of string from the eaves to the ground, and then measure the length of the string. Work out the combined area of the doors and windows and deduct this figure from the total.

If you are going to paint the pipes and the outside of gutters, multiply their circumference in centimetres by their length. Divide this figure by 10,000 to give an area in square metres.

Which paint to use In general, use exterior grade gloss paint on wood and metal – gutters, downpipes, windows and doors – and use exterior grade emulsion or masonry paint on walls. Alternatively, on bare wood you can use microporous paint, which needs no primer or undercoat. This paint allows trapped air or moisture to evaporate, reducing the risk of flaking.

You do not have to use a paint similar to the one previously used, but never put gloss paint over surfaces (mainly pipes and guttering) that are coated with bituminous paint. This tends to be less shiny than gloss and often looks thicker and softer than other paint. If you are doubtful about whether old paint contains bitumen, rub a rag soaked with petrol over the surface. If the rag picks up a brownish stain, the paint is bituminous. Either continue to use bituminous paint or, providing the surface is sound, coat it with aluminium primer-sealer, then paint with undercoat and gloss.

Paint the house in this order

Complete all the preparatory work before you do any painting – but never leave a surface exposed. Protect it with at least a primer and, if possible, an undercoat before you stop work at the end of a session.

Always decorate from the top of the house downwards so that the newly painted surfaces cannot be spoilt. Paint doors and windows last. Most professional decorators work in the following order, but if you are working from a scaffold tower you may wish to paint all the surfaces you can reach before moving the tower to another site. Try to keep on painting a wall until you reach a natural break.

1 Bargeboards, fascias and soffits

All these surfaces are painted in the same way, but not necessarily at the same time. Gutters are usually painted the same colour as fascias so it is easiest to paint them immediately afterwards – before soffits, which are often painted to match the walls or windows.

• Apply knotting, if necessary, and primer to bare wood. Put on an undercoat and leave to dry. Use two undercoats if there is to be a colour change.

• Lightly sand with fine abrasive paper to remove any rough bits.

• Apply a coat of gloss with a 75mm paintbrush, finishing with the grain. Leave it to dry for at least 12 hours.

• Apply a second coat of gloss.
As an alternative to new gloss over old, a stain finish designed to be applied over gloss paint gives a finish resembling natural wood. No base coat or primer is necessary.

2 Gutters and downpipes

Whether you paint gutters and pipes together or at different times, follow the same painting procedure for both.

• Clean out debris and wash with water and detergent.

• Remove rust from the insides of metal gutters with a wire brush. Wipe the surface with a dry cloth and apply rust inhibitor or metal primer. Paint the inside of gutters with any left-over gloss paint.

• Paint gutters and pipes with exterior gloss using a 50mm brush. If there is to be a colour change, apply one or more under-coats first. If the surface is coated with bituminous paint apply two thin coats of solvent-based (or synthetic) gloss paint.

• Hold a piece of cardboard behind pipes as you paint them, to protect the wall.

• Apply a second coat of paint when the first is completely dry.

Plastic gutters and pipes do not have to be painted, but if you want them to match a colour scheme, apply two coats of exterior grade gloss. Do not use a primer or undercoat. Manufacturers usually advise against painting new plastic because the paint will not adhere perfectly to it. After about a year it is safe to do so.

If you are leaving plastic gutters unpainted, unclip and remove them while you are painting the fascia boards.

3 House walls

• Treat new rendering which has not been painted before with a stabilising solution or a primer recommended for such a surface by the manufacturer.

• On painted rendering – such as pebbledash, spar dash or a textured surface – no undercoat is necessary. Apply two coats of exterior grade emulsion or masonry paint with a 100mm or 150mm paintbrush or an exterior grade shaggy pile roller. If you use a brush, work the paint into the surface with the tip of the bristles.

• Paint the area close to door and window frames with a 50 or 75mm brush.

• Do not try to paint the whole width of a wall along a house in one go. Instead, divide each wall into sections and paint one section at a time. If you cannot finish painting a wall in one session, stop at a corner of a feature – a window, for instance – so that joins will be less noticeable. Never stop in the middle of a wall. It will leave a noticeable mark.

• Wrap a collar of paper as protection around a newly painted pipe if you are painting the wall behind it. Move the paper down the pipe as you paint.

• Work safely at high levels, ideally with a helper to steady ladders and pass tools.

4 Brick walls

• Avoid painting good facing brickwork – it is difficult to achieve a satisfactory finish and cannot be successfully cleaned off later.

• If you really want to paint it, use exterior grade emulsion and a rough surface paintbrush. Apply at least two coats.

• To clean dirty bricks, scrub them with a hard bristle brush and plenty of water. Never use soap or detergent because they create permanent white stains.

5 Windows

If a concrete sill is damaged, repair it before painting the window frame.

• Strip paint off wooden sills and make them good, filling holes and uneven areas with exterior grade wood stopping or epoxy-based filler. Prime bare wood, then gently sand and wash with sugar soap.

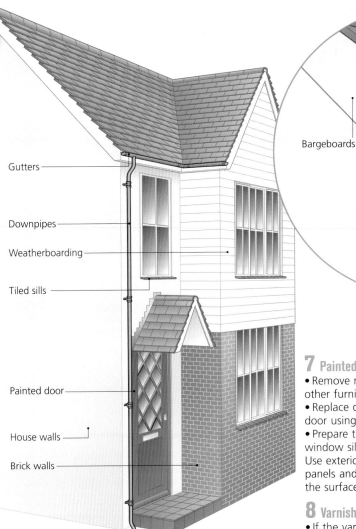

Bargeboards

Soffit

Fascia

Gutters

Downpipes

Weatherboarding

Tiled sills

Painted door

House walls

Brick walls

• To prepare metal frames remove rust with wire brushes and fill with epoxy-based filler. Then clean down with sugar soap and water, key with fine abrasive paper and apply a metal primer.
• Apply knotting to knots and resinous patches in bare wood. Then apply primer, undercoat and exterior grade gloss with a 25mm, 50mm or angled cutting-in brush.
• Take special care to seal the joint between putty and glass with new paint. This will prevent rain seeping through the window.

6 Tiled sills
• Clean window sills made of clay tiles with a fine wire brush; wash away the dirt with water and dry with a cloth.

Alternatively Clay tiles can be painted with special tile paint which is available in a limited colour range. No primer or undercoat is needed. Apply two coats with a 50mm paintbrush. The mortar joints may be painted or left natural.

7 Painted doors
• Remove metal handles, knockers and other furniture before painting.
• Replace damaged putty in a glass panelled door using a hacking knife or old chisel.
• Prepare the surface as for wooden window sills (see opposite).
Use exterior grade gloss to finish; paint panels and mouldings first, then the rest of the surfaces.

8 Varnished weatherboarding
• If the varnish is in good condition, rub over the surface with a flexible sanding pad damped with water to remove the glaze. Wash down with clean water, allow the surface to dry and then apply new varnish.
• If the varnish is in poor condition, strip it off using a varnish remover. Brush on a wood preservative and then varnish.

9 Painted weatherboarding
• Prepare as for wooden window sills (see opposite). Apply knotting, if needed, then wood primer, undercoat and two coats of exterior gloss paint. Alternatively, use microporous paint suitable for exterior wood.
• Work from the top down, and from left to right if you are right-handed and from right to left if you are left handed.
• Paint sections about 1m long at a time, using a brush just narrower than the width of one board.
• Paint the edge of the timber first, then the face, finishing with strokes that go with the grain.

DIY in the garden

Planning an area of decking

Decking has become very popular as a surface for garden terraces. Fairly easy to lay, it is a light job compared to alternatives such as paving and concrete patios. Specialised tools are not required but the work will go faster if you can arrange a helper, especially when setting posts and handling the joists.

Decking materials

If a deck is to last for a substantial period of time, it is essential that the timber is treated to stave off fungal attack and general deterioration caused by repeated wetting and drying. Timber can often be bought pressure-treated: in other words, preservative has been forced into the grain using specialised equipment at the sawmill. This treatment gives the best protection for timber that is in contact with, or close to, the ground. Alternatively, brush or spray on preservative during or after installation.

It is possible to order certain types of wood from timber merchants and decking specialists. Here are some of the types of wood available:

Softwood

Western red cedar Straight grained with an attractive smell; but has a tendency to split and dent; can be used without any treatment; very durable but soft.
Spruce Straight grained with few knots; use for out-of-ground components only.
European redwood Clearly visible grain; avoid the lower grades because they have lots of knots.
North American Douglas fir Yellow in colour with prominent grain; heavy and durable especially when treated.
British/European larch Avoid boards with lots of knots; can be expensive.
Southern yellow pine Visible grain with few knots.

Hardwood

Hardwoods are generally more expensive but will often be durable without the benefit of pressure treatment.
Teak Very durable with high strength; mid-brown colour; the king of woods for decking but very expensive.
Iroko Coarse grain, but not very visible; similar in appearance to teak but not quite so durable; brown to beige colour.
European oak Broad, straight to wavy grains; durable but expensive.
Opepe A popular choice for decking; an insignificant grain with a light brown colour; very durable.
Jarrah Straight grain and not strongly marked; dark brown.

Decking boards and tiles

Decking boards should be at least 50mm thick to combat the twisting and warping caused by repeated wetting and drying.

Ready-made wooden 'tiles' are a good alternative. Up to 1m square, they can be laid on a supporting framework to form a surface deck.

Planning consent

Generally you do not need planning consent for a deck in your garden but there are exceptions. You may need permission if your house is in a conservation area, listed, or in an area of outstanding natural beauty. If you are at all unsure, a phone call to the local authority planning officer could save you having to demolish your deck because you have contravened planning codes.

Points to consider

Decking boards come in widths ranging from 75mm to 150mm. The wider boards are faster to lay because fewer are needed. They often have a grooved surface that provides grip underfoot in wet weather and helps surface water drain away.

Building a deck is generally straightforward, providing a methodical approach is adopted and you plan properly before starting work. Construction techniques vary little, whether a deck is free standing or attached to some other element in the garden. Often decks are attached to the back of the house.

Look at the planned site for your deck in relation to the rest of the landscaping in the garden and take into account any other elements that may influence the design. Look at magazines, web sites and other gardens for ideas. Consider the neighbours: will the deck be so high that you overlook your neighbour's garden? Will you have privacy when you use your deck?

MEASURING UP

To work out the amount of timber required for the job, begin by measuring the width and length of the area to be decked. Then plan the layout of the supporting framework on paper.

You need to form a straight-sided frame around the perimeter and fix transverse joints across it – every 400mm if using 25mm wide thick decking boards, or every 600mm for thicker boards. For joists over 3m long, fix transverse braces every 2m to prevent warping. Work out the number of joists you need to cover the area, and calculate the amount of timber you will need for the whole framework.

For the decking boards, find out the width and length of the boards available, then calculate the number of boards you require.

Building a deck over paving

The simplest type of deck is built directly on top of an existing area of paving – concrete, paving slabs or pavers. This must be flat and mainly level, with a very slight drainage slope away from the house.

Tools *Measuring tape; pencil; panel or circular saw; paintbrush; cordless drill with twist drill bits and screwdriver bits; spirit level; string line; mitre saw.*

Materials *75 x 50mm timber joists; clear wood preservative; 75mm and 63mm zinc-plated countersunk screws (decking screws can be bought); 100mm masonry bolts; packing materials such as pieces of wood or slate; decking boards; decking sealer or stain.*

1 Cut the timber into lengths to create the supporting framework. Brush cut ends with preservative and butt together in position. Drill pilot holes, then secure each butt joint using two 75mm screws. Fix joists and any transverse bracing timbers in place. Check that the framework is square and level, with a slight fall for drainage.

2 If you need to secure the frame to the house wall, use 100mm masonry bolts.

3 Fix the transverse joists in position (see Measuring up, page 59, for how to space them). Wedge packing material under any part of the frame that is unsupported due to unevenness in the existing paving.

4 Cut the first decking board to length and lay it in place across the supporting framework and transverse joists, aligning it with one long edge. To improve drainage and ensure even spacing between the boards, use nails, pieces of card or wood spacers to leave a 5mm gap between boards, removing and re-using the spacers as you fix each board in place.

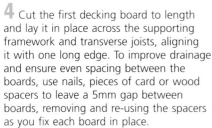

5 Using a power drill, screw two 63mm screws through the board over each joist and into every section of the outer framework. Use a string line to help you to align the screws across the deck's width. Cut the remaining boards, varying the lengths if you wish to stagger the ends, and fix in place in the same way.

6 You may have to cut the final board down in width to fit it in position. Set a circular saw to match the width required. If sawing by hand, clamp the board to your workbench and tackle a metre at a time. Get a helper to support the end of the board as you work your way along it. Fix the board to the frame in the usual way. Seal or stain the deck if needed or desired.

Constructing a raised deck

Over bare earth, support decking with vertical posts set into the ground and secured either with in-ground concrete collars (as below) or using metal fence post spikes.

Before you start Nothing spoils the sight of a new deck more than weeds growing up through the cracks between its boards. Therefore, before constructing the deck all vegetation, including turf, must be cleared. Compact and level the ground, leaving a gentle slope towards the outer edge of the deck to allow for drainage. Then lay a weed-suppressing membrane over the surface and cover with gravel.

Tools *Drill; saw; screwdriver; try square; spade; spirit level; tape measure. Power tools such as screwdrivers and saws will reduce the workload with some of the repetitive tasks.*

Materials *Concrete blocks for posts to rest on; cement, sand and aggregate; decking boards (plain or grooved), 100 x 25mm; joist hangers and galvanised nails; stainless steel screws, countersunk; 12 x 175mm galvanised bolts, nuts, and washers; wooden joists, 150 x 50mm, length depending on size of deck; wooden posts, 100 x 100mm, length depending on height of deck; decking boards.*

1 Use string lines pulled tightly between wooden pegs driven into the ground to mark out the edge of the site that will be covered by the deck. If the deck is to be oblong or square, measure the diagonals. When both diagonals are identical, the deck is a true square or oblong.

2 If the deck is going to be attached to the house, screw or bolt the wall plate to the building, ensuring that the top surface is at least 150mm below the level of the damp-proof course.

3 Mark out the centres of the joists at 300mm intervals from each end on the wall plate and nail on the joist hangers. You may need to alter the spacing slightly if the length is not divisible by 300.

Anatomy of a raised deck

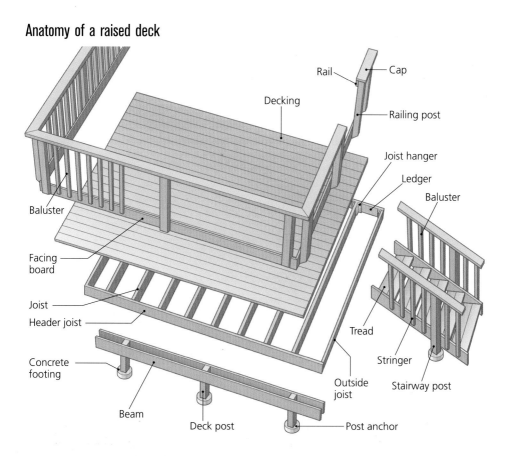

- Rail
- Cap
- Decking
- Railing post
- Joist hanger
- Ledger
- Baluster
- Baluster
- Facing board
- Joist
- Header joist
- Tread
- Stringer
- Concrete footing
- Stairway post
- Beam
- Outside joist
- Deck post
- Post anchor

4 Dig out holes 300mm deep and 300mm wide where the posts are going to go. There should be a post at each corner and one no more than every 2m across the deck. Place a concrete building block in the bottom of each hole and rest the base of a 100 x 100mm post on it.

5 Use a spirit level to ensure the posts are upright, nail temporary braces to the posts as support, then fill the holes with concrete, packing it tightly around the base of the posts.

The concrete should be a mix of one part cement, two parts sand and three parts aggregate. Double check that the posts are vertical and in line with your setting-out string, then leave them for 48 hours for the concrete to harden before continuing with the job.

6 Nail the two outside joists to the end of the wall plate, or ledger, reinforcing the corners with wooden blocks. Check that the joists are level, then drill and bolt the other end of the joists to the supporting deck posts.

You may find it easier to leave the joists a little too long and then cut them flush with the outside of the deck posts when you have fixed them in place.

7 Fix the front joist – the header joist – in place. Securely bolt it to the deck posts before trimming it flush with the outside faces of the outer side joists.

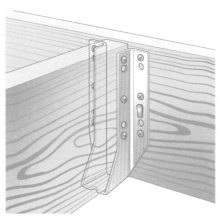

8 Nail joist hangers (above) to the inside of the header joist at identical spacing to those that you used on the wall plate, or ledger joist.

9 Cut all the joists to length, then drop them into the joist hangers and nail them in place.

10 Cut and fit the decking boards at right angles to the joists, using two screws where each board passes over a joist. Using a power screwdriver or a variable speed cordless drill, screw the boards down, 25mm in from each edge. Use a try square to make sure that each piece of decking is accurately positioned at right angles to the joists.

11 Start adjacent to the house leaving a 5mm gap between each board. Use nails, card or wood as spacers between the boards, removing and reusing the spacers as you fix each board in space.

12 If the deck is high enough to require a handrail, attach a rail to the inside of the posts 1m above the deck surface. Cut the top of the posts level with the handrail.

Building a pergola

A simple wooden pergola can be easily assembled, though the task is made easier if two people are working together.

Tools *Sledgehammer; spirit level; chisel; mallet; spanner; drill.*

Materials *For a pergola 4m long, 2m wide and 2.2m high, 100 x 100mm timber treated with preservative, as follows: 6 upright posts 2.7m long; 2 bearers (main beams) 4m long; 5 cross beams 2.2m long; 80mm screws; 200mm screws or carriage bolts; 6 metal post spikes.*

1 Mark out the area where the pergola is to be sited. Using short lengths of timber, mark positions for the posts, three on each side, and spaced 1.5m apart each way.

ANCHORING POSTS WITH CONCRETE

If you are building a heavy structure, or erecting a pergola on a light soil, where it might be loosened in high winds, it will need a firm foundation. Bed the upright posts in concrete footings rather than using metal spikes.

1 Dig a hole for each post with a narrow spade. Make the holes about 300mm square and 600mm deep.

2 Place a layer of gravel 100mm deep in the bottom of each hole to aid drainage and prevent the bottom of each post from rotting.

3 Mix up concrete using one part cement, two parts sand and three parts aggregate, in a wheelbarrow or electric mixer. Aim for a slightly dry mix that will support the posts better than very wet concrete until the concrete hardens.

4 Set the posts in the holes and get a helper to shovel in the concrete while you check with a spirit level that the posts are vertical. Work the wet concrete around the posts with a wooden stake to compact the wet concrete and work out any air bubbles.

5 If the posts will not stay upright on their own or if it is windy add temporary braces to hold the posts vertical until the concrete hardens.

6 After 2 to 3 days remove the temporary braces. Ensure the concrete has set hard before continuing with the construction of the pergola.

2 Drive metal post spikes into the ground to support the squared timber uprights. Use a sledgehammer and protect the top of the spike with a wooden 'dolly' (which can be bought) or a suitably sized offcut of timber.

3 Wedge the posts in the metal spikes and tighten the two bolts on either side to secure each one; check they are vertical.

4 Position a bearer along the top of the posts on one side of the pergola with an equal amount overhanging at each end. Using a spirit level check that it is horizontal. Mark the position of three posts on the bearer and the two midway points between the posts.

5 Using a chisel and mallet, cut out five halving joints at these marks, 100mm wide and 50mm deep, to house the cross beams. Do the same for the other bearer. Mark and cut corresponding halving joints in the cross beams, again allowing for an equal overhang of about 150mm at each end.

6 Set the bearers in position, together with the three cross beams that join them, over the tops of the posts. Drill through the joints and use 200mm screws or carriage bolts to fix them to the posts. Join the intervening two cross beams to the bearers with 80mm screws.

7 Finally paint or stain the completed pergola with your choice of finish, making certain that it is not poisonous to plants and animals. You may also want to add some screw-in vine eyes and plastic covered wire to encourage plants to grow over the completed structure.

Erecting an arbour

If you have room to build one, creating an arbour can provide a shady seat with a completely different view of the garden. Traditionally, the sides are covered with latticework to support climbing plants.

Tools *Tape measure; hand or power saw; power drill plus twist drill bits; try square; screwdriver; hammer; nail punch; trimming knife; sanding block and abrasive paper; pencil and string; paintbrush.*

Materials *For an arbour about 1.5m wide, 600mm deep and 2.4m high, preservative-treated softwood as listed, right. Also countersunk wood screws; panel pins; roofing felt and clout nails; exterior PVA woodworking adhesive; preservative wood stain.*

USING POST BASES

If you are erecting your arbour on a paved surface or a concrete base, you can use bolt-down post bases to support it. Once you have completed the basic framework (step 3), set each post in the shoe of its base and get the whole assembly perfectly square. Drill and plug the fixing holes, insert metal sleeve anchors and bolt each base down. Then replace the frame and secure each post in its shoe.

Making the frame

1 Cut the 75 x 25mm front and back seat rails and the three 75 x 38mm linking seat rails to length. Glue and screw them together to make the seat frame.

2 Screw the seat frame to the posts so the top of the frame is about 450mm above ground level. Attach two posts first, then get a helper to support the frame while you attach the other two posts. Check that the frame is square to the posts.

3 Stand the assembly upright and nail offcuts to the tops of the posts to keep it square. Screw the three cladding support rails to the rear faces of the back posts – one at the top, one about 300mm above ground level and the third in between.

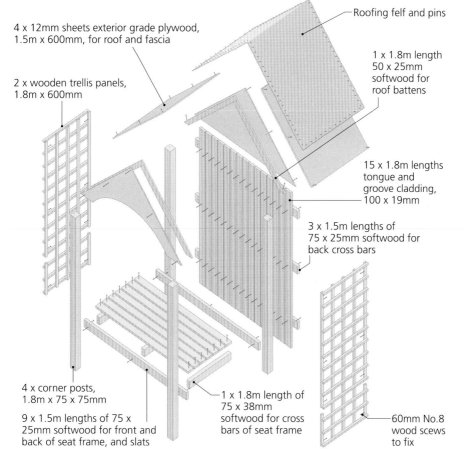

4 x 12mm sheets exterior grade plywood, 1.5m x 600mm, for roof and fascia

Roofing felt and pins

2 x wooden trellis panels, 1.8m x 600mm

1 x 1.8m length 50 x 25mm softwood for roof battens

15 x 1.8m lengths tongue and groove cladding, 100 x 19mm

3 x 1.5m lengths of 75 x 25mm softwood for back cross bars

4 x corner posts, 1.8m x 75 x 75mm

1 x 1.8m length of 75 x 38mm softwood for cross bars of seat frame

9 x 1.5m lengths of 75 x 25mm softwood for front and back of seat frame, and slats

60mm No.8 wood scews to fix

What you will need This diagram shows all the components you will need to build an arbour 1.5m wide, 600mm deep and 2.4m high – large enough for two people to sit comfortably side by side.

Cladding the frame

1 Fix the cladding to the support rails plank by plank. Slide the grooved edge of each one over its neighbour's tongue and tamp it down from the top to get it level.

2 Pin the first plank to the rails through its face and punch in the pin heads. Pin subsequent planks through their tongues so the fixings are concealed when the next plank is fitted.

3 Cut and fit the six seat slats. Fit the front and rear slats against the corner posts, then space the others out evenly using a slat offcut as a spacer. Fix the slats to each rail with two countersunk screws.

4 Complete the arbour frame by adding a 1800 x 600mm lattice trellis panel at each end of the structure. Set each panel between its posts, drill clearance holes through its sides and screw it to the posts.

Adding the roof

1 Cut two gable ends from a 1500 x 600mm rectangle of 12mm plywood and sand the cut edges. Draw a curve on the front panel (below) and cut it out.

DRAWING A CURVE

To draw a curve 1200mm wide and 280mm high, mark the apex of the curve (A) 280mm above the baseline. Measure 600mm from A to the baseline to find the two foci of the ellipse (B). Drive in a small screw at each focus and tie a loop of string round them so a pencil held in the loop rests at A when the string is taut. Move the pencil round the loop to draw the outline of the ellipse.

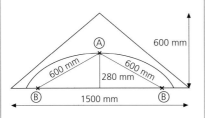

2 Glue and screw 50 x 25mm bearers to the top edges of the inner face of each gable. Glue and screw two plywood roof slopes to the top edges of the gables to complete the roof structure. Sit the roof assembly on top of the posts and drive a long screw vertically down through the roof into the top of each upright.

3 Cut a piece of roofing felt to cover the roof and fix it in place with clout nails. Add bargeboards to conceal the felt edges on the gables if you wish.

Children's play areas

Creating a safe play space in your back garden is a good idea if you have children. Take a look at the garden and see which parts you could incorporate into play areas – trees for tree houses or a sturdy branch from which to hang a swing.

You do not have to spend a fortune for your child to have a play area in the garden. If your child is old enough, involve him or her in the planning of the play area.

A secure space
One of the most versatile play areas is also one of the cheapest – a flat open area where children can run, ride bikes and generally let off steam. If there are trees, so much the better: these provide shade and encourage inventive and imaginative play. To keep your children in one place, it is

wise to have a fence or wall around the play area. Although many gardens already have walls and fences, consider a supplementary fence if your garden is large. You must also fence in pools and ponds.

Laying a safe play surface

You can minimise the risk of bumps and bruises by creating a soft surface underneath a swing, or on which to stand a climbing frame. The simplest surface is a thick layer of forest bark chips.

Tools *Scissors or sharp trimming knife; mallet; perhaps a saw; screwdriver.*

Materials *Weed membrane large enough to cover play area; edging material (such as fixed log edging, available in DIY stores); stainless steel screws; bark chips (the number of bags needed depends on area).*

1 Determine the shape and size of the area you wish to create and lay out your chosen edging. Make sure that it extends far enough around the climbing frame to break the fall of a child falling off.

2 Once you are happy with the layout, fix the edging in place. Hammer posts straight into the lawn then join the sections of edging using stainless steel screws. Lay out the weed membrane within the play area. It does not need pegging as the bark will keep it in place.

3 Rake bark chips in a thick layer (at least 50mm) over the membrane. This surface is low maintenance – all it needs is raking occasionally, and topping up with bark.

Making a sandpit

All children love sand. Here is an alternative to the bright plastic versions sold in toy shops. It has a lid to keep out rain and animals when not in use. Be sure to use playpit sand – builders' sand will stain clothes and is usually too coarse for play.

Tools *Hammer; drill with wood bits; saw; string and pegs; border edging tool; spade; screwdriver; tape measure; pencil; staple gun (or hammer and clout nails); abrasive paper.*

Materials *Eight decking boards; four 50 x 50mm sawn timber posts (about 350mm long with pointed ends) for corners; decking screws; sheet of weatherproof 12mm ply for lid and corner seats; three lengths of 50 x 25mm timber for lid lip; 2 x 2m sheet of butyl pond liner; six or more bags of playpit sand.*

The sandpit made here is 1200mm square and the depth of two decking boards

1 Decide on the position of the sandpit. Try to site it out of direct sunlight as the sand will reflect UV light, increasing the risk of sunburn. Push in a peg at each corner and stretch string all the way round. Then use an edging tool to cut through the turf along the lines to a depth of about 50mm.

2 Use a sharp spade to cut away the turf and remove the soil to a depth of about 50mm. Make the bottom as level as possible, digging out roots and stones.

3 Hammer the corner posts into the ground to the depth of two decking boards from the bottom of the excavation.

4 Measure the exact distance between the posts before sawing the decking boards to length; the boards will form butt joins at the corners. Drill pilot holes in the decking boards and, using decking screws, fix the boards to the posts.

5 Tip half a bag of sand into the hole and level it to make a smooth surface for the pond liner. Lay the pond liner in the sandpit and fill it with sand *before* trimming it to size – the weight of the sand will pull the liner further into the hole.

6 Trim the liner allowing an overhang of about 50mm all round. Then fold this under to make a neat hem and staple it to the exterior of the decking boards. Don't worry about all the creases in the corners – these will be hidden by the corner seats.

7 Cut four right-angled triangles from 12mm ply with the short sides about 350mm long. Sand the cut edges to get rid of splinters; drill pilot holes and screw them onto the corners of the sandpit.

8 To make a lid, measure the exterior dimensions of the sandpit and cut a square of plywood 50mm larger all round. Fix 50 x 25mm lipping to three sides of the lid and attach two handles to the side opposite the one with no lip. This will allow you to slide the lid on and off rather than lifting it – it will be heavy.

Installing a greenhouse

Position your greenhouse away from overhanging branches and where it will get the greatest amount of sunlight, particularly during winter.

Mark out where the greenhouse will stand, making sure you have a firm foundation of the correct size and type. It is important that the foundation will be able to support the structure you have chosen, and is dry and level. It may require a brick or concrete foundation. Some greenhouse kits come with their own base, which must be anchored to the ground through pins set in concrete. Have the holes dug and concrete ready.

Tools *Spirit level; ratchet or spanner.*

Materials *Greenhouse kit; ready-mixed concrete. Possibly washing-up liquid.*

1 Lay out the base frame and bolt it together on the firm, level area where the greenhouse will stand. Make sure the frame is square and sink the metal anchors into the concrete-filled holes.

2 Identify and lay out on the ground the two ends of the greenhouse framework, before bolting them together.

3 Next, lay out and assemble the sides of the greenhouse framework, bolting them together loosely. With a helper, lift the back and one side of the greenhouse onto the base and hold them in position while you bolt them together, making sure the corner is square.

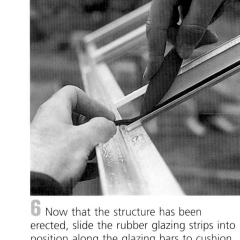

6 Now that the structure has been erected, slide the rubber glazing strips into position along the glazing bars to cushion the glass. A small amount of washing-up liquid applied to the glazing bars helps the strips to slip into place.

4 Bolt the second side and the front of the greenhouse onto the first two sections, with a helper holding them steady. Then fasten the sides and ends onto the base.

5 Fix the ridge bar of the roof into place and slot in all the roof bars.

7 Start glazing the structure with the glass or plastic sheets supplied. It is easier and safer to work on the roof first, before doing the sides. Fasten the glass to the glazing bars using the W-shaped glazing clips supplied.

8 Finally, assemble and glaze the door, checking that it will open and close smoothly. Once this is done, tighten the bolts of the entire structure.

Putting up a shed

A garden shed can have a variety of uses, from simply being a place to store garden tools to acting as a backyard hobbies room or workshop. Sizes vary so choose one that is large enough to cover future as well as present needs. Consider the siting of the shed carefully, particularly if you plan to run electricity to it.

Putting up a kit shed

Putting up a shed is often achievable in a few hours, but all but the smallest tool stores come in large sections, so you may need to enlist some help putting it together. Even the most basic of sheds can be greatly improved by adding some additional felt to the roof to ensure the interior stays dry.

If the shed is to be used as a workshop or hobbies room consider installing insulation within the interior timber framework and cladding the inside with plywood or hardboard for a smooth finish. Some sheds come prefinished but most arrive as bare wood in which case you will need to paint on some sort of protective finish or wood preservative.

Tools *Tape measure; power screwdriver; power drill with twist and countersink bits; pencil; spirit level; try square; trimming knife; straightedge; hammer.*

Materials *Shed kit. Possibly also additional roofing felt.*

1 Unless you are erecting your shed on a level hardstanding, you will need to create a firm and level base for the structure before you start. You can do this by laying several paving slabs on the site of the shed and spanning them with timber fence posts, running at right angles to the bearers on the shed's floor and spaced no more than 750mm apart. Make sure that all the slabs are level with one another, so that the shed will sit square on its base.

Alternatively A sturdier option would be to lay an area of concrete, slightly smaller all round than the footprint of the shed, so that rainwater running off the shed will drain away into the ground.

2 Start by lifting the gable end into position and propping it upright with a post. The bottom batten of each panel should sit on the shed base, so that the panel boarding extends beyond the base.

3 Lift a side panel into place and screw it to the gable end where the frames meet. Put three fixings at each joint, at the top, middle and bottom of the panel.

4 Complete the walls by fitting the two remaining sides. The shed should balance on the base, with the panels lipping over the floor and the battens resting on it. Do not screw the walls down to the floor yet.

5 If the shed kit includes a beam to support the roof, fix it across the shed from gable end to gable end. This will also help to brace the structure.

6 Fit the door into its opening and check that it opens and closes easily. If it doesn't, the shed may not be quite square. Loosen the roof beam and check each corner with a try square. Hammer the corners to square them up if necessary, using an offcut of timber to protect the panels of the shed.

7 Lift the roof panels into place and secure them to the roof beam, if there is one. Screw through the roof into the sides and gable ends, too, to hold the roof firmly in position. Nail the completed structure to the floor of the shed.

8 Cut the roofing felt supplied with the shed into three equal pieces: one for each slope of the roof and a third to lay over the apex, overlapping each side panel by at least 75mm. Allow for an overhang of 50mm at either end.

9 Use felting nails to tack the felt in place, starting with the side panels. Space the tacks 300mm apart along the top edge of the felt and 100mm apart along the gable ends and the eaves. Lay the middle length of felt over the apex and nail it in position all round.

10 Make neat folds at the corners (see Re-felting a pitched shed roof, right) then hammer the fascia boards into place. Nail decorative fillets, if supplied, to the apex of each gable end.

11 Nail strips of corner trim onto each corner of the shed to finish the structure, then fix a sliding bolt or hasp and staple to make the door secure.

Re-felting a pitched shed roof

If there is visible damage at several spots on a shed roof, or if water leaks through in places even though you can see no damage, the bituminous felt covering needs replacing.

Before you start Bituminous felt is sold in green, black and red, and in various grades; the heavier the felt, the longer it lasts.

You will usually be able to reach the top of the roof working from a stepladder and moving it along as necessary. If you cannot reach from a stepladder and are not sure that the roof will bear your weight, get someone to help you.

Tools *Stepladder; claw hammer; sharp knife; wooden batten about 1m long; old paintbrush. Possibly also a chisel, plane and screwdriver.*

Materials *Wood preservative; bituminous roofing felt; 13mm galvanised clout nails; chalk; cold felt adhesive. Possibly some new softwood boarding or some outdoor grade plywood or chipboard; fascia boards, ridge board or eaves battens with galvanised nails or screws for fixing.*

Preparation

1 Tear off all the old felt. Prise out any old nails with the claw hammer. If any heads break off, hammer the shanks down flush so that there are no sharp projections to damage the new felt.

2 Check the timber covering of the roof for damage or rot, and replace it where necessary. Saturate any replacement wood with preservative and let it dry before use.

If a plywood or chipboard sheet needs replacing, unscrew it and screw a new one in its place with galvanised screws.

If a tongued-and-grooved board needs replacing, cut through the tongue with hammer and chisel so you can ease the board out. You will not be able to fit a tongued and grooved replacement, unless you remove the tongue. Alternatively, you can plane down a piece of softwood to fit the gap exactly. Nail it in place with galvanised nails.

3 Where a fascia board, ridge board or eaves batten is damaged or missing, fit a new one. Treat it first with preservative and fix it with galvanised screws or nails.

4 Treat the remaining roof timber with preservative and let it dry.

5 Cut the felt into strips of the right length with a sharp knife. The strips should run parallel to the ridge and overlap the roof by 25mm at each end.

Fixing the felt in place

1 Position the first strip with its lower edge overlapping the eaves by 25mm and its ends overlapping the fascia boards by 25mm at each end. Run the wooden batten along it – from the centre towards the ends – to smooth out wrinkles. Using 13mm galvanised nails, nail the top edge of the felt to the roof timber at 150mm intervals and the bottom edge to the outside face of the eaves batten at 50mm intervals. Nail the ends of the felt strip to the outside of the fascia boards at 50mm intervals.

2 At the corners where the eaves and the fascia boards meet, fold the surplus felt into a neat triangle, bend it flat and drive a nail through it.

3 Chalk a line along the length of the felt strip 75mm below its top edge.

4 Brush a strip of adhesive onto the top edge of the felt, taking it down to the chalk line. Take care not to let it spread below the line or a black smear will show on the felt. Leave the adhesive for about 30 minutes to become tacky.

5 Position the next strip of felt carefully over the adhesive. Run the batten over the felt from the middle to the ends to smooth it out. Press down the overlap firmly.

A two-slope shed roof

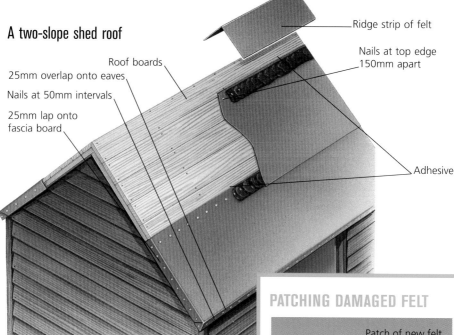

Ridge strip of felt

Nails at top edge
150mm apart

Roof boards

25mm overlap onto eaves

Nails at 50mm intervals

25mm lap onto
fascia board

Adhesive

6 Nail the top edge at 150mm intervals and the ends at 50mm intervals.

7 If the slope is big enough to need another strip of felt, lay the next one in the same way. Leave up to 380mm unfelted at the top.

8 Repeat steps 1–7 to felt the other slope of the roof.

9 Measure the gap from the top of the felt on one side over the ridge to the top of the felt on the other side. Measure in several places. Take the highest figure, add on 150mm and cut a strip of felt this width and the length of the ridge plus 50mm.

10 Lay the felt in place, centred over the ridge, and make a chalk line along each edge to show where to put adhesive. Put the felt to one side.

11 Brush strips of adhesive about 75mm wide along each slope. Do not let adhesive spread below the chalk lines. Leave the adhesive to become tacky.

12 Lay the felt in place on the adhesive on one slope. Press it down firmly, then smooth it over the ridge and press the other edge in place. Run the batten over the felt on both slopes from the centre outwards to drive out air.

13 Nail the ends to the fascia boards at 50mm intervals. At the top angle, fold the surplus felt over neatly and drive a nail through the fold.

PATCHING DAMAGED FELT

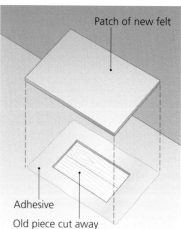

Patch of new felt

Adhesive

Old piece cut away

If a small area of felt is damaged, you can patch it with a felt off-cut and cold felt adhesive.

1 Cut out a rectangle of felt that will cover the damage and extend beyond it by at least 75mm all round.

2 Position the patch over the damage and run a piece of chalk around the edge to mark the area for the adhesive.

3 Brush the adhesive over the marked area with an old paintbrush. Do not let it spread outside the chalked area or smears will show on the roof. Leave the adhesive for 30 minutes to become tacky.

4 Lay the felt patch in position and press it down firmly from the centre to the edges to make sure no air bubbles are trapped under it.

Planning a fence

• In a windy spot, an open fence such as post and rails would offer little wind resistance. However, a solid fence would need to be very sturdy. Any solid fence higher than 1.2m is at risk of being blown down, no matter how well it is constructed, so it would be best to use open trellis to add any extra height.

• If the level of the neighbouring garden is higher and so the outside of a fence would be in contact with earth (which rots timber), consider building a fence on a low brick or block retaining wall, with gaps for concrete spurs to support timber fence posts.

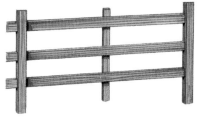

Post-and-rail (or ranch-style or railboard) Spaced horizontal rails secured to posts. Rails may be square sawn, half round, or rustic (poles, often with the bark intact). Rails (usually three) can be nailed or slotted into posts, which are usually about 1.8m apart. Height range from 300mm to 1.8m, but normally about 900mm – three rails. Suitable for a boundary or for decoration. Not as expensive as closeboard or panel fencing, and not much affected by wind. The timber needs regular painting or preservative treatment (page 83).

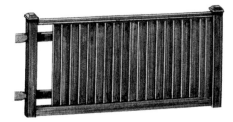

Closeboarded vertical Upright, overlapping feather-edged boards (tapered on one side) nailed to horizontal arris rails. Boards are about 150mm shorter than the post height above ground, to allow for a horizontal gravel board. Posts are usually 2.4m apart. Excellent for screening or security, but expensive. Wood needs regular preservative treatment (page 83) to prevent shrinking or rotting. A fence has to be buillt up from separate timber components.

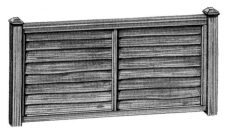

Panel Ready-made panels fixed between posts. Panels may be thin interwoven slats, overlapped horizontal boards, or vertical closeboard. Panels are normally 1.8m wide; narrower sizes are made to order. Height range: 600mm–1.8m. Easy to put up, and good for screening or security. The timber needs regular preservative treatment to prevent shrinkage or rotting. Quality varies – poorly made panels are likely to distort.

Closeboarded horizontal Horizontal boards nailed between posts. The boards are either feather-edged overlapping, or shiplap (with a step-shaped overlap). No arris rails or gravel boards are used. Posts are usually about 1.2m apart, with 2.4m boards butt-jointed on alternate posts. More posts are needed to give the fence strength than with vertical closeboard, making the fence very solid but a more expensive choice.

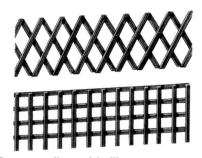

Square or diamond trellis Square trellis is usually made from hardwood battens forming squares of about 150mm, and can be bought in ready-made sections about 2m wide and 300mm–2m high, or as panel fencing. Diamond trellis is often expanding, and sold in 1.8m lengths with a height range of 300mm–1.2m. Sections can be fixed above each other. Rustic diamond trellis (not expanding) is also available.

Palisade or picket Spaced, upright stakes nailed to horizontal rails slotted into posts. Posts are usually about 2.4m apart, and the height range is about 900mm–1.2m. Fencing can be bought in ready-made sections about 1.8m long, with brackets supplied for fitting sections to posts. Suitable for a boundary fence. Comparatively cheap. Can be painted or treated with wood preservative (page 83).

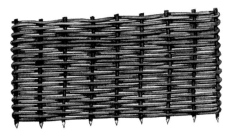

Hurdle or wattle Thin or half-round interwoven rods formed into 1.8m wide panels that can be supported on stakes or between posts. Osier (willow) rods form hurdles, hazel rods form wattles. Height range is about 600mm–2.1m. Not very long-lasting, but useful as a temporary screen for protecting growing plants. Hurdles are more expensive than wattles.

Cleft chestnut paling Stakes wired together and stretched between posts. End and corner posts are usually braced with stays. Posts are usually about 2.7m apart, and the height range is 750mm–1.8m. Suitable for a temporary boundary – while a hedge is growing, for example. Easy to put up and take down. Needs no maintenance but wires must be tensioned if the fence is to stay taut.

FENCE POST ACCESSORIES

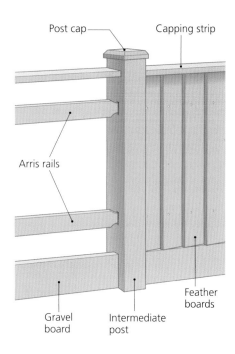

Post cap — Capping strip

Arris rails

Gravel board — Intermediate post — Feather boards

Timber post Usually softwood such as larch or pine. Buy posts ready-treated with preservative, preferably by vacuum/pressure impregnation although this is more expensive. Posts are available with ready-cut mortises for arris rails. Post sizes are normally 75 or 100mm square.

Timber post cap Flat or bevelled timber cap that is necessary for shedding rainwater and preventing rot.

Capping strip Wooden strip nailed across the top of vertical closeboard fencing to protect the vulnerable end-grain from rot.

Gravel board Board, usually made of wood or concrete, that is fitted across the base of a fence to protect the rest of the fence from rot caused by contact with damp ground.

PLANNING PERMISSION

You must have planning permission to put up a fence more than 1m high if it fronts on a public road, or to put up any fence more than 2m high.

Putting up fence posts

If the distance between fence posts is critical – for example, when fitting ready-made panels – erect posts in pairs and fit the fencing as you go.

• It is advisable to buy new posts that have been pre-treated with preservative.
• Timber posts can either be concreted in or bedded in a mixture of well-compacted hardcore and soil. Concreting ensures a more solid and durable fixing, especially on soft ground, but may slightly increase the risk of rotting.
• Concrete posts must be concreted in.

Preparation

• For fences over 1.2m high, sink the bottom of the post at least 610mm below ground – or 760mm for tall concrete posts.
• For lower fences, sink timber posts 460mm, and concrete posts 610mm.
• Timber posts should have about 150mm of hardcore below them to provide drainage and lessen the risk of rotting.
 The distance between posts depends on the type of fence. If the new fence replaces an old one and you want to put the posts in the same positions, you will have to dig out the stumps of the old posts, and possibly the concrete surrounding them. Alternatively, you can install a half panel or short section of fencing at each end of the fence so that the new posts fall midway between the old positions.

Tools *Post-hole borer or narrow spade – unless using spikes; string and pegs; spirit level; one timber length longer than the distance between posts; one timber length as long as the distance between posts; timber lengths for temporary post supports; mallet; hammer; timber length or earth rammer (page 90). Possibly also demolition hammer or pickaxe; sledgehammer; chalk.*

Materials *Posts of treated timber or concrete; hardcore (page 88); 50mm or 75mm fence nails. Possibly also fast-set bagged dry mix or concrete foundation mix – about one bucketful per hole; bolt-down post base.*

1 Mark the inside line of the fence by stretching the pegged string along its length.

2 Use the timber length to measure the distance between each hole, and cut out the area of each hole with a spade. Make a chalk mark instead if the fence crosses a solid surface.

3 Fix the first post to the wall, if necessary (see page 76).

4 If a hole has to be made in a patio, either take up a slab or the bricks, or break a concrete surface with a demolition hammer, and dig below.

5 Using a post-hole borer or narrow spade, dig each hole to the required depth; remember to include an extra 150mm for hardcore beneath a timber post. Keep the hole as narrow as possible for the size of the post.

6 For a timber post, fill the base of the hole to a depth of 150mm with hardcore, well rammed down.

7 Insert a post so that one side is against the string guideline, and pack some hardcore round the base to keep it upright.

8 Lay a length of timber across the top of each pair of consecutive posts and use a spirit level to check that the tops are level.

9 Use a spirit level to check that the post is vertical, then pack in more hardcore to support it.

10 To give a stronger temporary support, drive a nail into the post and wedge a length of timber under the nail as a brace.

11 Fill in the hole as soon as the fence has been erected. Either fill it with layers of hardcore and a mixture of soil and gravel, ramming the surface well down, or fill the hole with alternate layers of hardcore and concrete rammed well down. Slope the top layer of concrete round a timber post so that rainwater runs off away from the post.

Fixing a timber post to a wall

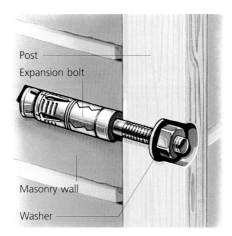

Post

Expansion bolt

Masonry wall

Washer

A post fixed against a wall usually rests on the surface of a path or patio, so should be cut shorter than the other fence posts by the amount they are to be buried below ground. Soak the sawn end with wood preservative overnight (page 83).

Secure a post over 1.2m high to the wall with three equally spaced expansion or anchor bolts at the top, middle and bottom. For shorter posts use two bolts. Each bolt should be twice as long as the

width of the post, as half will be sunk into the brickwork. For panel fencing, the bolt heads must be recessed to lie flush with the edge of the post. On any type of fence, it is neater and safer if they are recessed.

Tools *Steel tape measure; chalk; power drill and two auger bits – one of the bolt-hole diameter, one wide enough for the nut recess, allowing for use of a spanner (or use a flat bit for the recess); masonry bit of the recommended diameter for the expansion bolt shield; spirit level; 100mm nail; hammer; box or socket spanner to fit bolt nut.*

Materials *Sawn post; two or three projecting-type expansion bolts – for fixing about 60mm thickness.*

1 Use a steel tape measure and chalk to mark the hole positions on the post.

2 Drill holes of suitable diameter through the post at each marked point, then make a hole for the nut recess about 15mm deep.

3 Hold the post in position against the wall and use the spirit level to check that it is vertical. Then insert a 100mm nail through each hole and tap it with a hammer in order to mark the hole position on the wall. Avoid mortar joints if possible.

4 Remove the post and drill holes in the wall of the correct diameter for the bolt shield, and to the depth the bolt will be sunk into the masonry. Remove debris from the hole.

5 Insert the sleeves and bolts (with nuts and washers removed) into the wall holes. Hang the post on the bolts and replace the washers and nuts. Tighten the heads with a box or socket spanner.

CONCRETE SHORT CUTS

To fix a fence post quickly, you can use Supamix Post Fix, which sets in about 10–20 minutes, instead of using rubble and cement. It is sold in 25kg Maxi-Packs, each sufficient for erecting one fence post.

Fixing panel fencing to posts

Put up posts in pairs as described on page 75. You will need a helper to lift and support large panels.

Before you start Fix each panel to its first post before positioning the second post. The fixing method depends on whether you are using nails or fence clips on timber posts, or fitting panels into slotted concrete posts. Fit a gravel board in the same way as for a closeboard fence (see page 79). If you are not using gravel boards, each panel must be fixed about 75mm off the ground, or it will quickly rot.

Tools *Power drill; wood bits; hammer. Possibly also screwdriver; two or three bricks; timber lengths for supporting panels; G-cramp.*

Materials *Posts – one more than the number of panels; panels; either nails (twelve 50mm or 75mm galvanised or alloy nails per panel) or fence clips (four per panel, with sufficient screws or nails for each clip). Annular (ring-shank) nails give the best grip. Possibly also one 1.8m gravel board for each panel; post caps.*

Nailing panels direct to posts

1 Drill pilot holes for the nails in each panel. Make six holes each end – three on each side through the inner face of the panel frame at the top, middle and bottom. Drill the holes right through.

2 Hold the panel in position against the first post (use a G-cramp if working alone). Allow enough space at the bottom of the post for fitting a 150mm gravel board, or rest the frame on bricks to leave a gap of 75mm.

3 Nail the panel to the first post, driving the nails in at a slightly upward or downward angle so that they will not pull straight out if the fence comes under pressure at a later date.

4 Position the second post with the other end of the panel butted to it. Ensure the post tops are level (opposite). Nail the end of the panel in place and concrete the post.

Using fence clips

Drill starting-holes for nails or screws that are to be driven into the panel frame, otherwise the wood could split.

Some clips are two sided with a post-fixing screw welded to one side. Screw the clips to each post before fitting the panel against it. Place a clip at the top and bottom of each post, facing opposite ways so that each side of the panel is supported. Nail each clip to the panel after fitting it.

Some clips are three sided, with no built-in screws. Screw them to the post before fitting the panel.
   Some clips wrap round one side of the panel frame. Fit them to the top and bottom of the panel on opposite sides of the frame before fitting the panel and nailing the clip to the post.

Fixing closeboard vertical fencing to posts

This type of fencing is excellent for both screening and security, but the timber needs regular treatment to prevent shrinking or rotting.

Before you start Posts can be timber or concrete, and are available with ready-made slots (mortises) for arris rails. Some concrete posts have recesses to which the rails can be bolted. Posts for corners are usually wider than intermediate posts, and are mortised on two adjacent sides.

• Put up posts (page 75) in pairs, fitting arris rails between them. Make sure the posts are the right way round. Some posts are recessed on the bottom front edge to accommodate the gravel board, which fits directly below the overlapping feather-edged boards. The back of the fence is the side on which the arris rails are visible. Rails are normally 2.4m long, and after they have been slotted into the posts, the length to which boards can be fitted is about 2.3m.

• Use upper and lower arris rails for fencing up to 1.2m high, and an extra central rail for a higher fence. Rails may be supplied square sawn and need shaping.

Tools *Spirit level; hammer; block of wood about 90mm wide as a width gauge. Possibly also panel saw; wood plane or shaping tool; power drill with wood bits.*

Materials *Posts – one for each 2.4m section and one extra; two or three arris rails for each section; four 50mm galvanised or alloy nails for each rail; feather-edged boards treated with preservative (probably 27–29 between posts); two 50mm galvanised or alloy nails per board; one 2.4m gravel board for each section. Possibly also capping strip and nails; clips for fixing gravel boards.*

Fitting arris rails

1 With the end post in position (page 75), insert one shaped end of each rail into the post to the full depth of the slot.

SHAPING AN ARRIS RAIL

Use a panel saw to roughly shape the two short sides of the triangular rail so they slope down to a flat stub of the same width as the fence slot. The third, widest side of the rail – to which the boards are nailed – should remain flat. Plane the surfaces smooth until the stub fits neatly into the slot to the required depth.

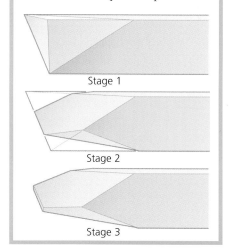

Stage 1

Stage 2

Stage 3

2 Hold the second post in position while you fit the other ends of the rails into the post slots to half the depth of the slot (for intermediate posts, there will be a rail fitted in from each side).

3 Support the post temporarily with timber braces while you level it with the first post and check also that the arris rails are horizontal.

4 Adjust the post as necessary before concreting it in.

5 Nail the arris rails to the posts, driving one nail at an angle through the top of each rail and the other at an angle through the bottom of the rail.

6 Continue fitting posts and rails in the same way until the skeleton of the fence is complete.

Fitting feather-edged boards

1 Fit the first board with its thicker end butted against the post. Nail it to the centre of the top arris rail, driving the nail at a slight sideways angle.

2 Use a spirit level to check that the board is vertical before driving in the bottom nail – and the central nail, if there is one.

3 Place the width gauge on the first board, aligned with the thick edge, and fit the second board against it. The thick end of the second board should then overlap the thin end of the first board by 15mm.

4 Nail the second board to the rails, driving each nail through both boards at a slight sideways angle.

5 Continue fixing boards in the same way, checking continually that they are vertical.

6 Before fitting the last three or four boards, measure the gap still remaining to see whether you need to decrease or increase the overlap to fill the rail.

Alternatively Maintain the 15mm overlap and fill the last gap with a board fitted backwards – that is, with its thick end butted to the end post.

Fitting a gravel board

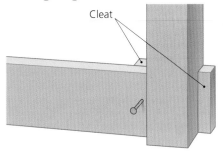

Cleat

One way of fixing a gravel board between timber posts is to nail small wooden cleats to the foot of each post, then nail the gravel board to the cleats. Alternatively, boards can be trimmed to fit between the posts and fixed with gravel-board clips.

Fitting a capping strip

A wooden capping strip is nailed across the top of vertical closeboard fencing to keep it straight and prevent it from rotting or snagging.

1 Saw off the fence posts level with the top of the fence boards. If the capping strip is not wide enough to completely cover the post tops, either fit a cap to each post (page 74), or slope the uncovered part.

2 Treat the exposed parts with wood preservative (page 83).

3 Place each capping strip to stretch from the centre of one section, across a post to the centre of the next section, with strip ends butted.

4 Nail the strip to the top of a post with 50mm galvanised or alloy nails.

5 Use 25mm nails to nail the strip to board tops at each end, and at one or two places in between. Take care not to split the boards. If you find that the nails are splitting the wood, drill a pilot hole for each nail.

Fence repair and maintenance

All wood is susceptible to rot and attack by wood-boring insects, so treat fences and other garden woodwork with wood preservative regularly to prolong their life.

Timber rots in contact with earth, so whenever possible keep it from direct contact with the ground. Never pile soil against a wooden fence. Timber fence posts are most likely to rot at the bottom below ground, and will eventually collapse and bring down part of the fence unless reinforced in good time. To prevent a post rotting from the top downwards, slope the top or fit a post cap (page 74).

Featheredged boards often get brittle and start to crack if they are not kept well protected with wood preservative. So do arris rails, which take a lot of strain in supporting featheredged boards or palings, and will quickly get worse unless repaired.

Reinforcing a fence post

If the main part of a rotting post is still sound, it can be supported with a concrete spur. Alternatively, it can be cut short and refitted with its base in a metal post spike. If the rot extends higher than the top of the gravel board, you will have to free the fencing from the post on either side before you can cut the rot out. It may be simpler to replace the post.

Tools *Handsaw; old paintbrush; timber lengths for fence supports; timber length for compacting concrete; spade; hammer; drill and 13mm auger bit; spirit level with horizontal and vertical vials; spanner; hacksaw.*

Materials *Wood preservative (page 83); concrete spur; two 10mm diameter coach bolts about 200mm long; nut and washer for each bolt; concrete foundation mix.*

1 Temporarily support the fence on each side of the post with pieces of timber.

2 Remove the gravel board and cut off the rotting part of the post back to sound wood.

STOP POSTS ROTTING

Even pre-treated posts will benefit from some extra protection. Soak the part of each fence post that will be buried in the soil, in wood preservative (page 83) for 24 hours. Lean the posts against a wall in separate containers, or in an improvised trough, such as a shallow pit lined with a thick sheet of polythene. Pour wood preservative into the bottom of each container. It is not usually practicable to immerse the full 460 or 610mm of the post, so brush the preservative up onto the posts from time to time. Allow posts to dry for 24 hours before using them.

3 Coat the whole post, especially the bottom and end grain, with wood preservative.

4 Dig out a hole alongside the damaged post to a depth of about 450–600mm. Make the hole at least 300mm square.

5 Put the spur in the hole, fitted snugly against the post.

6 Slip coach bolts through the holes in the spur and strike them firmly with a hammer to mark their positions on the post.

7 Remove the spur and bore holes through the post at the marked spot.

8 Push the bolts through the post and spur so that the tails are on the spur side. Slip on the washers and nuts and tighten the nuts with a spanner.

9 Use a spirit level to check that the post is vertical, pushing it upright as necessary. Then brace it firmly with lengths of timber.

10 Ram hardcore into the bottom of the spur hole, then pour in the mixed concrete, pressing it well down with the end of a piece of timber.

11 Wait 24 hours before moving the timber supports, to give the concrete time to set. Use a hacksaw to cut off protruding bolt threads slightly proud of the nuts.

Replacing a timber fence post

Tools *Pincers or claw hammer; narrow spade; spirit level; length of timber longer than distance between posts; timber lengths for supporting post; earth rammer (page 90). Possibly also timber length; nails; strong rope; pile of about five or six bricks.*

Materials *Treated fence post the same size as the old one; hardcore (page 88) – probably 3–6 bucketfuls; two or three arris-rail brackets (see page 82); 50mm galvanised nails.*

HELPFUL TIP

If a post is difficult to remove, or if it breaks off and leaves a stump, lever it out using a length of timber and a large stone or a pile of bricks about 300mm high. Lash one end of the timber length to the post or stump, and lay the timber across the stone or brick pile as a fulcrum (balancing point).

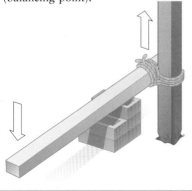

1 Support the fence on each side of the post with lengths of timber, wedged under the panel top or upper arris rail.

2 Free the post from the fencing. Undo panels by removing the nails or clips on each side. For vertical closeboard fencing, remove the first board on one side and saw through the arris rails. Remove nails holding the rails to the other side of the post so that they can be pulled out when the post is moved.

3 Dig down beside the post to free it at the bottom. Then remove the post and clear the hole.

4 Fit the replacement post in the same way as putting up a new post (page 75), but on a closeboard fence, fit the shaped arris rails into the slots on one side as you put the post in. Before you fill in and firm the hole, make sure the fencing will fit flush on both sides.

5 Refit sawn off arris rails to the post using metal arris-rail brackets, but nail shaped arris rails (page 82). Refit panels with nails or clips (page 77).

6 If the post top is square cut, either cut it to a slope or fit a post cap (see below). Treat sawn areas with wood preservative.

Repairing a post top

Before repairing the post, probe the top with a sharp knife to find out the extent of the rot. Saw off the rotten area back to sound wood.

Timber or metal post caps are sold ready made. Soak a home-made wooden cap in wood preservative for 24 hours before fitting. The cap should be about 15mm wider than the post top all round. Nail it to the post with two ring nails driven in on the skew – at an angle from each side.

A metal post cap can be home-made from a sheet of zinc or aluminium cut about 25mm wider than the post top and turned down round the edges.

Mending a cracked arris rail

Strengthen a rail cracked in the middle with a straight arris-rail bracket – a metal bracket about 300mm long, shaped to fit the rail, with ready-made holes for screws or nails. Fasten it with galvanised or alloy 25mm screws or 50mm nails.

If the crack is near a post, use a flanged arris-rail bracket. The two flanges – projecting lugs at right angles to the bracket – are fastened to the post. If the post is concrete, use screws and wall plugs to fasten the flange to the post.

Tighten a loose arris rail by pinning it with a 10mm grooved hardwood dowel about 50mm long. Drill a hole for the dowel through the front of the post about 20mm from the edge where the loose rail fits. Before inserting the dowel, coat it all over with waterproof adhesive.

Replacing a broken arris rail

If the fence posts are concrete, they may be fitted into mortises in the same way as timber posts, and can be repaired as described here.

Tools *Panel saw; hammer; plane or shaping tool; pencil.*

Materials *Arris rail, normally 2.4m long, treated with wood preservative; flanged arris-rail bracket (see left); 50mm galvanised or alloy nails.*

1 Hammer the boards or palings away from the damaged rail.

2 Withdraw the nails if possible and pull the damaged rail from the slots at each end. Otherwise, saw through the rail flush with the post at one end.

3 Shape one end of the new rail to fit into the post slot (page 78). Fit the new rail into the slot, mark where it will fit flush against the post at the other end, then saw it to length.

4 Refit the rail into the slot, and fix the other end to the post using the flanged bracket. Refit the boards or pales to the rail, making sure they are vertical.

Replacing a gravel board

If for any reason a rotting gravel board cannot be replaced without dismantling the fence – if it slots into concrete posts, for example – nail the new board to timber battens fitted beside the posts.

Remove the damaged board by drilling and sawing through flush with the posts at each end. Treat the new gravel board and the timber battens with wood preservative at least 24 hours before fitting them.

For timber posts, use 150mm battens, which can be nailed to the posts. For concrete posts use battens 600mm long, drive about 450mm into the ground beside the posts, as near as you can.

Dig a shallow groove under the fence to make way for the new board. Fix the battens so that the board can be fitted flush with the front of a closeboard fence, or centrally under a panel fence. Support the battens from behind while you nail the gravel boards to them. Keep soil away from the board as much as possible.

Replacing a panel

Fence panels are made in standard sizes, so removing a damaged panel and fitting a new one in the same way (page 77) is not usually difficult.

If the new panel is slightly too wide, plane off a small amount of the frame on each side. If, however, it is not wide enough, close the gap with a narrow fillet of wood inserted between the post and the panel frame. Remember to treat the wood fillet with preservative before fixing it.

Repairing feather-edged boarding

Replace damaged or rotten boards with new boards that have been treated with wood preservative (see right).

One nail secures two overlapped boards, so to remove a board you will have to loosen the overlapping boards as well and pull out the common nail. Fit the new boards as on page 79.

Undamaged boards sometimes become loose because their nails have rusted. Refit the boards using 50mm galvanised or alloy nails that will not rust.

If feather-edged boards are rotting at the bottom where there is no gravel board, saw them off along the base to leave a gap of at least 150mm. Then cut and fit a gravel board (page 79).

APPLYING WOOD PRESERVATIVE

Coat existing timber fences with wood preservative regularly, particularly any joints or end grain.

Choices
A wide range of wood preservatives is available. Most modern preservatives are either solvent-based or water-based, and contain chemicals or salts that destroy fungi and insects. Solvent-based types give off flammable fumes, and naked flames should be kept away until the preservative is quite dry – until at least 12 hours after application. Look for a warning on the container. Water-based types have no smell. Neither type is harmful to plants once dry, but guard against splashing any on plants while you are painting.

Application
The period between treatments depends on the type of wood preservative used and how exposed the fence is. Most modern preservatives will last 2 or 3 years.

Even if timber for a new fence has been pre-treated with preservative by the manufacturer, ideally by a vacuum/pressure process, coat it with more preservative before you fix it in place and thoroughly soak cut ends.

The best time to apply preservative is when the wood is thoroughly dry but the sun not too hot – probably in late summer after a dry spell, with no rain expected for a day or two. Damp wood will not absorb the preservative well.

Apply preservative with an old paintbrush or a garden pressure spray. Or there are kits on the market which pump the liquid from the container to a brush. Always follow any safety precautions given on the container.

Coverage is generally around 4–10m^2 per litre, but varies with the type of preservative and the porosity of the wood. Treated wood can then be painted the colour of your choice, but many brands contain colouring.

Methods of hanging a gate

There are three main ways in which a gate can be hung from timber gateposts. The method depends on the types of fitting used.

Flush between posts

The gate is hung between the posts, with the back of the gate flush with the back of the posts.

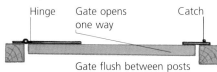

Hinge   Gate opens one way   Catch

Gate flush between posts

This is the usual method of hanging a timber garden gate with flush-fitting hinges. The gate opens one way only. The clearance for fittings on each side of the gate needs to be about 5mm.

Centred on posts

The gate is hung between posts, with the gate width centred on the gatepost width.

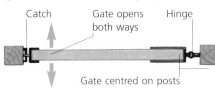

Catch   Gate opens both ways   Hinge

Gate centred on posts

This method is common with wrought-iron gates, which usually hook onto a pin, and with double-strap hinges on timber gates. The gate will swing both ways unless there is a stop on the fastener. Depending on the type of catch, the clearance on the hinge side may need to be as much as 100mm, and on the catch side about 55mm.

Hung behind posts

The gate is hung on the back of the posts with an overlap of 15–25mm on each side. This method can be used for a pair of gates, or a wide single gate, hung with a standard hanging set.

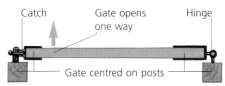

Catch   Gate opens one way   Hinge

Gate centred on posts

The gates can swing inwards only, and slam shut against a post. The types of fastener that can be used are limited.

Hanging stile   Slam or swinging stile

Checking the design

Although some gates look the same from both sides, many have a supporting framework at the back. These types of gate should always be hung with their back on the inside.

Gates are often also designed for either right or left hanging. The hanging stile may be wider than the slam or swinging stile, to give a strong fixing for the hinges.

Wooden gates should be braced – by fixing a diagonal strut between the top and bottom rails of the frame – or they will sag over time. Where there is only one diagonal brace, the gate must be hung with the top of the brace on the closing side and the bottom of the brace on the hanging side. You can follow this convention when working out whether a gate is designed to be hung on the right or left.

Double gates must be a matched pair, designed for left and right hanging.

Fitting a gate between existing supports

1 If you can, buy a gate that is exactly the same width as the old one. Fix the hinges to the back of the new gate before you fit it. Wedge the replacement gate between the existing posts, raising it off the ground with a couple of offcuts of wood to ensure adequate ground clearance.

2 Check that the clearances are equal on both sides of the gate then mark the position of the hinges on the post. Screw the hinges to the post (left).

3 Hold the latch bar horizontal and screw the latch hook to the gate post and the latch.

4 Remove the wedges that are holding the gate in position and check that it swings freely and that the latch works smoothly. Adjust the positioning if necessary.

If you cannot buy a gate to fit
If you are not able to find a new gate in the exact size you need, you will need to adjust the size of the gate or the gap between the posts.

   If the distance between the existing timber posts or brick piers is too wide for the gate and fittings, narrow the gap by fitting timber battens on one or both sides. The gate fixings can then be fitted to the timber battens. Make sure that the battens allow sufficient clearance for the fittings. The gate can then be hung in the way described above. Fixings are also available for fitting gates directly to a masonry pier (see right).

Do not buy a gate until you are sure how wide you want it and how you are going to hang it. The width and fitting method are interdependent. Check also that the gate is designed to hang on whichever side you require – either right or left. If it is to hang across a sloping driveway, it will need to accommodate rising hinges – some types are self-closing.

   Gates are made in both metric and imperial sizes. Be sure you know the exact width, because conversions are inaccurate. The width range for both systems is generally similar.

   Single gates range in width from about 900mm to about 3.7m, increasing by increments of 300mm or 600mm. Double gates may range from about 4m to 6m wide. The height range is typically from about 1 to 1.75m, but gates as high as 2m and 2.5m are available.

If you cannot find a gate narrow enough to fit the gap between existing supports, you may be able to trim a little off both stiles of a timber gate to reduce its width. Otherwise you will either have to have a gate specially made or remove the existing gate supports and put up new ones, spaced farther apart.

Hanging a gate on masonry piers

Masonry piers are usually made of large blocks of cut or ashlar stone, or bricks. Although rough stone may be used this makes hanging a gate much harder. Drilling for the hinges will be easier if you start with a pilot hole.

Tools *Hammer; drill; masonry drill bits; spirit level.*

Materials *Eyebolt hinges; gate latch; gate.*

Before you start Check the piers to make sure that they are in good order before hanging your gate and make any necessary repairs to the masonry. Special hinges are needed for hanging a gate on masonry, so don't use hinges meant for wooden posts.

1 Place the gate between the two piers. When viewed from above the gate should bisect the centre line of each pier. Sit the gate on temporary packing so that it is about 50 to 60mm above ground level.

2 Place wedges on either side of the gate so that the gate is held firmly. Use the spirit level to make sure that the top rail is level.

3 Measure down 175mm from the top rail and 250mm up from the bottom of the gate on the hanging side and put a pencil mark at these points. Transfer these pencil marks to the masonry piers then remove the gate.

4 Drill a pilot hole, then a larger hole, for the hinge: the size is dependent on the hinges that you are using. Hammer in the plug and screw in the hinge.

5 Attach the other half of the hinge to the gate, check to make sure that it swings properly and that the gap is even. If it is not, screw the hinges in or out of the piers a little to adjust their position.

6 Finally attach the latch to the other side of the gate and the striker to the pier.

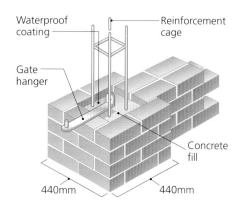

Waterproof coating — Reinforcement cage

Gate hanger

Concrete fill

440mm   440mm

Alternatively If you are building a pier to take a gate, set the gate hangers into the masonry as you work.

Hanging a pair of gates

Cramp double gates together and hang them in the same way as a single gate, but with a clearance gap between them. Use a strip of wood 15mm wide down the centre, and pack it out at the top to be 20mm wide, so that the gap is wider at the top. This allows for initial wear on the hinges, which would otherwise cause the gates to drop at the centre. Use two or three large G-cramps to hold the stiles together, making sure the two gates are level with each other.

FIXING A GATE POST TO A WALL

You can buy fixing brackets for securing a gate post to a wall or a masonry pier. They comprise right-angled brackets with bolts that are anchored in the wall and plugs that are anchored in the post. A post secured in this way will support the hanging or closing side of the gate.

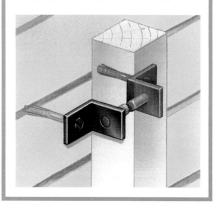

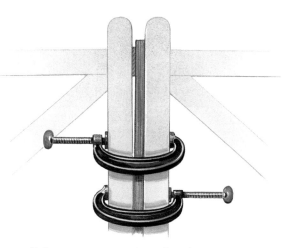

If the gates are cross-braced, make sure that the bottom of each diagonal is on the hinge side, so that the tops of the two diagonals meet in the middle.

Looking after a gate

Keep gates well treated with timber preservative or paint to prevent rotting or rusting. Hinges can be smeared with oil or grease to guard against rust, but for latches, which are constantly handled, paint is preferable, unless they are galvanised or japanned metal.

Repairing rotten timber

Cut out small areas of rot on the gate back to sound wood and fill the cavity with a two-part wood-repair filler of the epoxy-resin type. This sets after about 15 minutes and can be sanded down with medium-grade abrasive paper or a power sander to a smooth finish.

Rotting timber parts such as pales or braces can be replaced. Treat new timber with a wood preservative (page 83), using a clear coating if it is to be painted later, or buy pre-treated timber, which will last longer. A rotting or damaged gatepost should be replaced or repaired in the same way as a fence post (page 80); but do not use a post spike. Repair a rotting post top as you would a fence post top (page 81).

Dealing with rust

Keep a lookout for rust spots appearing on fittings or metal gates, and remove them with abrasive paper. Repaint the area you have rubbed down immediately – rust can recur overnight. Remove severe rusting by scrubbing with a wire brush (wear safety goggles). Do not use a proprietary remover if you are going to repaint with a rust-inhibiting paint. Once the rust is removed, you can either repaint the area with a rust-neutralising primer followed by an undercoat and gloss coat, or use a one-coat paint such as Hammerite, which is both a rust-inhibitor and a finishing paint.

Repairing a sagging gate

The most common cause of a sagging gate is hinges that have worked loose through years of use, so check the condition of the hinges first. Replace loose hinge screws with longer, galvanised screws if possible. If not, tap wooden dowels (or fibre wall plugs) into the holes and use screws of the same size.

Alternatively, if possible, refit the hinges slightly higher or lower so that the screws will be biting into firm wood. Replace worn or broken hinges.

If the hinges are in good condition, the timber joints of the gate may be loose. An isolated loose joint can be repaired by fixing a metal plate – tee, corner or straight – or an angle bracket to the joint. Try to force a waterproof adhesive up into the loose joint, then hold it together while you screw the bracket in place.

A very rickety gate should be either replaced or taken apart and remade. Clean away all old adhesive from the joints and reassemble using a waterproof adhesive. Reinforce mortise-and-tenon joints by drilling into the post and through the tongue of the tenon, then insert a glued dowel. After reassembling the gate, clamp it together while the adhesive dries.

A gate may sag because it has no diagonal brace, or because the brace is not strong enough (or the gate may have been hung on the wrong side). The brace should be firmly fitted between the cross rails on the back of the gate, with the top towards the latch.

Lift and wedge the gate into its proper position and make sure that it is a good fit before fixing the brace with waterproof adhesive and galvanised screws.

Preparing the sub-base for a path or patio

How well a surface will support heavy loads depends to a great extent on the strength of the sub-base.

THE SUB-BASE MATERIAL

Hardcore is made up of well-broken bricks, blocks or stone and can be bought from builders' merchants. A tonne of hardcore covers roughly 6m² if it is laid 100mm deep.

Some hardcore may contain demolition rubble, which includes unsuitable material such as wood and plaster. Such hardcore will not bed down well.

Gaps in the hardcore surface are filled with a thin layer of ballast (sand and shingle) – a process known as blinding.

Hoggin is a more expensive form of hardcore, made up of gravel and sandy clay, and will bed down well.

Before you start Some paving materials need a sub-base of hardcore only, others need hardcore topped with a layer of concrete. On soft ground or where heavy traffic is likely, the sub-base may need to be even deeper.

• If a hardcore sub-base is necessary for a path, set up string lines and marker pegs and dig out the site only to the depth of the surface material and any bedding needed, such as a mortar or sand layer. Slope the bottom of the excavation to one side and use a spirit level and shim across the bottom to get the required slope. Fill in any depression in the surface with well-broken hardcore. Use a garden roller to compact the surface until it is firm and even.

• For a patio, hardcore is only necessary below the surface material.

Tools *Pegs and string lines; builder's square; mallet; spade; shovel; steel tape measure; timber pegs 25mm square and 460mm long; chalk or paint; wheelbarrow; spirit level; wooden shims; earth rammer, garden roller or plate vibrator. Possibly also sledgehammer; concreting tools.*

Materials *Hardcore (see left); ballast. Possibly concrete.*

Four layers of a path The depth of the sub-base material depends on the surface it is supporting, the weight that will have to be carried, and the nature of the ground. This illustration shows a path in cross-section.

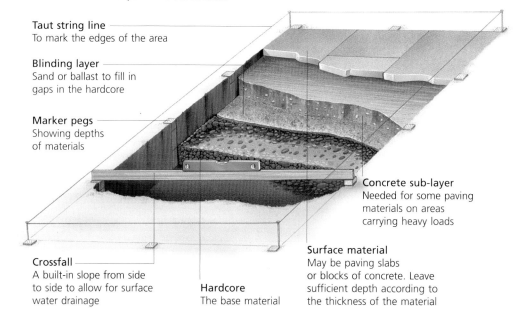

Taut string line
To mark the edges of the area

Blinding layer
Sand or ballast to fill in gaps in the hardcore

Marker pegs
Showing depths of materials

Concrete sub-layer
Needed for some paving materials on areas carrying heavy loads

Crossfall
A built-in slope from side to side to allow for surface water drainage

Hardcore
The base material

Surface material
May be paving slabs or blocks of concrete. Leave sufficient depth according to the thickness of the material

1 Use taut pegged string lines to mark the edges of the path or patio area, allowing for permanent edging. Check with a steel tape measure that the width of the site is uniform, and use a builder's square to ensure that right angles are true. For making a curve, see page 90.

2 Decide on the direction of the crossfall. A path need not slope along its length, but it should have a crossfall of about 1 in 80 away from the wall if it is alongside a house (see Making a sloped surface, right). For a patio, a slope of 1 in 60 away from the house or towards a drain is normally enough for drainage, but not so steep as to affect the levels of chairs and tables.

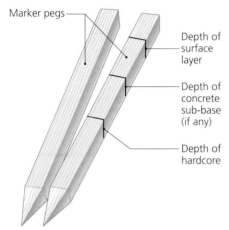

Marker pegs

Depth of surface layer

Depth of concrete sub-base (if any)

Depth of hardcore

3 Mark the timber pegs from the top to show the depths of the various layers, allowing for any bedding sand or mortar.

4 Drive a marked peg into the ground in the top corner (nearest to the house) of the area to be excavated. Set it with its top at the right level for the drive surface.

5 Drive in a row of pegs at about 1.5m intervals across the top of the site, using a spirit level between pairs of pegs to ensure a crossfall of 1 in 80 for a path and 1 in 60 for a patio (see panel, right).

6 Drive in a second row of pegs 1.5m farther down the path or patio. Set the top of each to allow for any lengthways slope necessary from the first rows – for a fall of 1 in 100 use a 16mm shim.

7 Continue with rows of pegs down the path or patio in this way at similar intervals, adjusting the distances of the last rows as necessary so that the final row is at the bottom edge of the site.

8 Dig out the area within the string lines to the lowest peg mark (the base of the hardcore layer). Spread the topsoil on other parts of the garden. Leave any clayey subsoil in a heap for later disposal.

9 Spread hardcore in the excavated area. Ram it down well – using an earth rammer or, for larger areas, a garden roller or plate vibrator – until it is at the marked level for the hardcore surface. If laying concrete paving blocks (page 94), break up the hardcore as small as possible with a sledgehammer before compacting it with a vibrator.

10 Add a thin layer of ballast to fill in the gaps. Ram it down well.

11 If the base material includes a layer of concrete, spread the concrete over the hardcore and blinding layer and tamp it down to the marked level.

12 Remove the pegs and fill in the holes with hardcore or hardcore and concrete before laying the paving material.

MAKING A SLOPED SURFACE

Place a spirit level – on a length of timber, if necessary – across the pegs marking the surface level. Use a thin piece of wood (a shim) under the spirit level, or its support, on the lower-side pegs. Tap down the lower-side peg until the spirit level is set level with the shim in position.

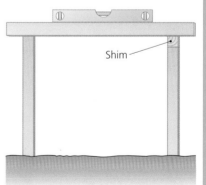

Shim

The thickness of the shim depends on the slope required and the width between pegs. For example, on a path 1m wide, you need a 13mm shim for a crossfall of 1 in 80, 16mm for 1 in 60, or 25mm for 1 in 40. The calculation of the shim size need not be precise.

Marking out a curved path

Use a garden hosepipe or lengths of rope to mark the outline of the curve on each side by eye.

It is usually necessary to allow extra width between the curving sides. If they are the same width apart as the straight sides, an optical illusion will occur, making the path appear to be narrow at the curve when viewed from a short distance away.

Set up a peg and string line to follow the shape of the marked curve. The pegs will need to be closer together than when using straight string lines.

TOOLS FOR LAYING A SUB-BASE

Many compacting or demolition tools can be hired. Hire firms are listed in *Yellow Pages* under Hire Services – Tools and Equipment.

Earth rammer A steel handle with a heavy club end for ramming down hardcore.

Garden roller A sand or water-filled roller 100kg or heavier to be used instead of an earth rammer for compacting large areas of hardcore (or for rolling cold asphalt surfaces).

Plate vibrator Instead of a roller, you can hire a petrol-driven plate vibrator (also known as a power compactor) for ramming down large areas of hardcore. It is also used for bedding down concrete paving blocks.

Demolition or breaker hammer The easiest way to break up a concrete surface before laying a new path or drive is with an electric-powered hammer. It is fitted like a drill with a chisel or point for cutting, and can also be used with a masonry bit for drilling fixing holes into or through concrete. Hire a lightweight tool for concrete up to 100mm thick, or a heavyweight one for thicker concrete. Wear safety goggles and, if possible, steel-tipped boots when using the hammer.

Other useful tools Pegs and a string line are needed for marking the outline of an area to be excavated. The stretched string line, held taut between the pegs, is also a guide for keeping straight edges.

A garden spade is necessary for digging out soil from the sub-base area. A sledgehammer may be useful for breaking up hardcore, and a pickaxe for breaking hard ground or small areas of old concrete. Both can be hired.

You will also need concreting tools if the sub-base needed includes a layer of concrete above the hardcore.

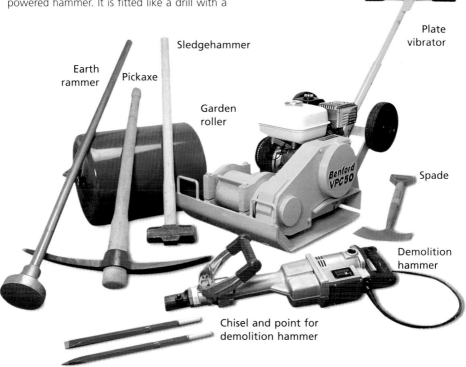

Plate vibrator

Sledgehammer

Earth rammer

Pickaxe

Garden roller

Spade

Demolition hammer

Chisel and point for demolition hammer

Choosing paving materials

There are many types of paving materials. All of the following are suitable for patios and paths. Only block paving is suitable for driveways. Whether natural stone flags or concrete slabs, most paving materials are heavy to handle. Some must be set in a mortar bed, while others can simply be laid on a bed of sand.

Natural stone

All natural stone paving should be laid in a properly prepared mortar bed. Many people choose to hire a professional for this job.
• Suitable for patios and paths
• Looks and is weathered
• Natural, beautiful finish
• Expensive to buy
• Must be laid on a mortar bed
• Joints must be filled with mortar

New sandstone, flagstones, travertine

• Natural product that improves with age
• Expensive to buy
• Must be laid on a mortar bed
• Joints must be filled with mortar

Pressed concrete

Many composite blocks are designed with DIY in mind. The slabs are often less heavy than stone and they are also less expensive. Some even come in setts, where each slab resembles a group of smaller ones, making laying easier. You can also buy slabs moulded to look like cobbles, individual cobblestones, or even a 'carpet' of cobbles, linked together with nylon – rather like sheets of bathroom mosaic tile.

Smooth or 'weathered' paving slabs

• Colours include grey, buff and red
• Square, rectangular, hexagonal and circular shapes available
• Reasonably quick and easy to lay on a straight site, but difficult to form into curves
• Can often simply be laid on a bed of sand and the joins filled with sand

Block paving
• Colours include grey, red, charcoal, brown, buff, marigold and red-grey mixtures
• Laid on a bed of sand and the joins filled with sand
• Blocks take longer to lay than slabs but are easier to fit into awkwardly shaped areas
• Large areas may be best tackled by a professional
• Specially designed circle or octagon packs (see right) available that will match your chosen patio slabs

Cobbles by the length
• Fitting very simple and quick
• Easy to cut, flexible mat, so unusual shapes can be filled by cutting and interlocking
• One typical version comes in 1200mm x 400mm sheets
• Can be laid on any surface – even grass, which grows up between the cobbles

Constructing a patio

A patio makes a useful sitting or dining area in a garden. Draw a scale plan on graph paper before you begin any work, so that you can work out positions of retaining walls or steps. Make sure your patio will not block any airbricks in the house walls.

Tools *String; wooden pegs; spade; rammer or wooden post; spirit level; heavy post or vibrating plate compacter; straightedge board or timber; spacers; brush; hammer or board and mallet; trowel.*

Materials *Suitable paving materials (page 91); hardcore or crushed stone (page 88); dry sand; mortar (page 99).*

2 Cover the excavated area with 100mm of hardcore or crushed stone, spreading it evenly until the surface is level.

3 Compact the hardcore with a vibrating plate compacter (which can be hired). For awkward corners, or a small area, use a heavy post to ram down the hardcore. Once this layer has been well firmed, cover it with about 80mm of dry sand. Use a board or plank with a straightedge to level and compact it.

1 Roughly mark out the patio area and clear it. Dig out the soil to a depth of about 150mm, then compact the base with a post or rammer. Measure and mark again, more accurately, using a string line and wooden pegs. Use a spirit level and pegs to establish the final level of the patio surface, ensuring it has a drainage slope (page 89).

4 Starting at a corner, set out the edging bricks in a stacking or soldier bond using a straight-edged plank to use as a guide. Insert spacers to keep the gaps even.

5 Bed the bricks onto a damp mortar mix (or a bed of sand) and use a spirit level to check them. Tamp the bricks into the mortar or sand, using a board and mallet or a hammer, until they are all level.

6 Bed the paving slabs. Spread more sand topped with dry mortar mix so that the slabs will be level with the surface of the bricks. Keep on checking the levels.

7 Sprinkle a dry mortar mix or sand over the bricks and slabs and brush it into the spaces between them. It will give a firmer finish and discourage weeds in the gaps. Make sure you fill the gaps completely.

8 When you have completed the whole area, brush off the excess sand or mortar. Allow the surface to settle for a day or two before walking on it.

Creating an optical illusion

Brick or paver patterns can be used to make the patio's dimensions look different. If bricks run lengthways they will give the impression of extra length; bricks running across a patio will make it look broader. Always keep patterns clear and simple, and avoid mixing them, for the best effects.

Granite setts, laid along the edges, finish off the paved area and provide a hard-wearing surface, unaffected by frost.

PATHS AND PATIOS

Laying block paving using a plate vibrator

Block paving needs to be well bedded to give a stable surface and carefully planned to create a pleasing finish.

Before you start The only way to lay a large area is with a plate vibrator, a light compacting machine powered by a petrol-driven motor. This compacts an area of blocks laid on sand to a level, rigid surface, compressing the sand bed from about 65mm to 50mm deep.

You can hire a plate vibrator. Ask for one suitable for compacting paving blocks. Pass it over the area as evenly as possible. Do not use it within 1m of an unsupported edge, where blocks are still being laid.

Where there is no adjoining wall or hard edge, lay edging blocks (right) or kerbstones otherwise the joints in the paving will open and the blocks spread.

Small areas can be laid without using a vibrator, although the surface will not be as stable. The sand layer will only need to be about 55mm deep. Before levelling the sand bed, dampen it until it holds together.

Tools *Straightedge; levelling strips of 65mm wide timber as long as the width of the area to be paved; shovel; rake; kneeling board; either block splitter (see opposite) or brick bolster and club hammer; plate vibrator; soft broom. Possibly also brick trowel; string line and pegs; builder's square (see right).*

Materials *Paving blocks, sharp sand – 1m³ covers about 15m² at 65mm deep. Possibly also edging blocks; foundation mix concrete; water.*

1 Prepare a hardcore base for a patio or path (page 88), wide enough to accommodate a concrete bedding strip for any edging needed (see right). Allow space above the base for the block depth and for a 50mm layer of sand (the depth after compaction).

2 Lay edging blocks if necessary (see right), allowing for the correct crossfall and any lengthways slope (page 89).

Wait three days for the bedding mortar to harden before laying the paving.

3 Place piles of bedding sand, kept as dry as possible, along the site at about 3m intervals so that you can spread it in sections without having to walk over it.

4 Lay 65mm levelling strips on edge across the site – one where you intend to start laying and one 1–2m farther down the site. Check their crossfall with a spirit level.

5 Spread the sand evenly between the strips, using a shovel and rake. Then lay the straightedge across the strips and use it to rake off excess sand until the surface is level with the tops of the strips.

6 Prepare two or three sections to give a 3–4m² run for laying. Remove the levelling strips as you go along, carefully filling the depressions with sand.

7 Start laying blocks at one corner of the prepared sand bed, but keep off the bed. As you work forwards, lay a kneeling board across the blocks already laid but not yet compacted.

MAKING A BUILDER'S SQUARE

Use three pieces of wood about 50mm wide and 19mm thick, each accurately marked with one of the following lengths: 450mm (A); 600mm (B); 750mm (C).

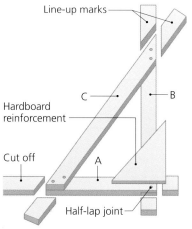

Line-up marks

Hardboard reinforcement

C   B

Cut off   A

Half-lap joint

Line up all the marks carefully before nailing lengths to each other. Use a half-lap joint for A and B, then overlap C. Check the right angle with a set square, saw off any overlap, then reinforce the corner with a piece of hardboard. (Any three lengths of wood joined in the ratio 3:4:5 must form a right angle.)

8 Lay the blocks snugly against each other according to the chosen pattern, leaving no joint gaps. Lay whole blocks first, and cut and fit part blocks later. Check corners with a builder's square (opposite). Blocks laid at the edges should stand about 10mm higher than the edging – they will bed down when compacted.

9 After laying a run of about 3–4m², use the plate vibrator over the area two or three times, but keep it at least 1m back from the last row of newly laid blocks. You can then see how much the blocks are bedding down. The actual amount depends on the moisture content of the sand. If the compacted surface is conspicuously too high or too low, lift the blocks and adjust the level of the sand bed.

10 Continue in this way until all the whole blocks have been laid. Then fill in the part blocks and compact the area again with the plate vibrator as before.

11 When all the blocks have been laid and compacted, make sure that the surface is dry, then spread a layer of dry, fine sharp sand on it. Use the plate vibrator to work the sand into the crevices between the blocks to lock them in position. Get a helper to brush sand towards the vibrator, as it will be forced away by the vibrations.

Cutting paving blocks

The easiest and quickest way to cut paving blocks is with a block splitter, a hand-operated hydraulic cutter that can be hired. The alternative is to cut them with a hammer and bolster in the same way as bricks (page 105) – a lengthy job when you are paving a large area.

Laying edging blocks

A common and reliable edging is a row of paving blocks on edge, bedded in stiff sand-and-cement mortar on a layer of concrete (page 99). Use the foundation mix. Allow 200mm space for each line of edging blocks at the edges of the area to be paved.
• Make the concrete layer 75mm thick and 300mm wide, to allow 75mm on the outside and 25mm on the inside of the line of edging blocks. Make the concrete surface at the correct depth to allow the top of the edging to coincide with the finished level of the compacted paving. Generally the depth is about 80mm to accommodate the 65mm deep block and a 20mm layer of bedding mortar.
• Wait 24 hours for the concrete to harden before laying the edging on a bed of 3:1 sand-cement mortar. Use a taut string line to set the surface level, taking into account the crossfall and any lengthways fall. Slope the bedding mortar a little way up the outside of the edging to make a small haunch. Leave no joints between blocks, unless the edging is curved.

For curved edging, use a stiff sand-and-cement mortar (2:1 mix). Make the joints 10–25mm wide and pack them with mortar one day after bedding the blocks. Use a little mortar at a time, packed in with a strip of plywood. Fill to the bottom of the chamfered edge of the block, and sponge off any that smears the surface of the edging.

After completing the edging, wait three days before laying the paving blocks. Check that none of the bedding mortar used for the edging will impede the levelling of the paving blocks. If necessary cut mortar away down to the 25mm ledge of the concrete bed.

LEVELLING THE SAND WITH A NOTCHED BOARD

Where the site has fixed edging on both sides – a footpath, for example – the sand can be levelled with a notched board rested across the edging. Use a length of 100 x 50mm board with a 150mm long notch at each end. To allow for the sand compaction, the depth of the board below the notches should be about 5mm less than the depth of the paving blocks, unless you are using a plate vibrator, in which case it should be about 15mm less.

Repairing paths, drives and steps

Small cracks that develop in the surface of a path or drive often result from errors in construction – weaknesses in the sub-base, for example, or faulty concrete mixing or misjudging curing times.

Before you start It is a waste of time to repair small cracks as soon as they appear. Wait to see if they increase in size and number. They may be caused by a small amount of movement in the ground below.

If, after a year or so, there has been little or no increase, it is fair to assume that the ground has settled and repairs can be carried out.

If the surface develops extensive cracking or sunken areas, take it up and lay it again on a new, firm sub-base.

Refitting a loose or damaged paving slab

1 Use a spade to chop through any mortar at edge joints. Push the spade under the slab to lift it and slip a broomstick or pipe under it to roll it out. A sunken or see-sawing slab can be re-laid, but renew a cracked or chipped slab.

2 If the slab was bedded on sand, loosen up the old sand with a trowel, add more sharp sand, and lightly level the surface with a length of wood.

Alternatively If the slab was bedded on mortar, remove the old mortar with a hammer and chisel. Mix new bedding mortar in a dryish mix of one part cement to four parts sharp sand (or use a bagged sand-cement mix) and spread it over the surface with a brick trowel to a thickness of 30–50mm. Roughen the surface with the trowel point.

3 Slab edge joints may be flush or with gaps. If there are gaps, place 10mm thick wooden spacers along one long and one short edge before rolling the slab into position on a broomstick or pipe. Then space other side gaps.

4 Lay a 50mm thick piece of flat wood on the slab as a cushion while you use a club hammer to tap it down flush with the surrounding slabs. Check that it is flush using a length of straight-edged timber.

MAKING A CONCRETE FILLER

Prepare a cement and sharp sand mix in the proportions 1:3 by volume, or for small amounts use a bagged sand-cement mix.

Separately mix equal parts of water and PVA adhesive – a building adhesive used to seal or bond various building materials is ideal.

Mix the dry material, water and PVA adhesive together until the filler is a smooth, moist consistency – neither crumbly nor too sloppy.

---

5 If you cannot tap the slab down flush, lift it again and skim off some of the bedding material. Or, if it sinks down too far, add more of the bedding material.

6 Wait at least two days before filling in the joints. Mix mortar to a dry stiff mix, using 1 part cement to 2 parts sharp sand. Force the mortar well into the joints with a piece of wood 10mm thick. Tap the mortar down so that it lies a few millimetres below the slab surface. Wipe off excess mortar with a damp sponge.

Cleaning up stains

Oil, grease and rust stains, or moss, often occur on paths and drives. Most can be removed with one of the wide range of proprietary removers available from DIY, gardening or motoring stores. Cat litter is a good absorbent for spreading on fresh oil spillages.

Renewing damaged kerbing

1 Use a club hammer to loosen the damaged length of kerbing, then prise it out with a spade.

2 Dig out about 50mm of the sub-base below the removed kerbstone, then ram the surface well down with a thick piece of timber.

3 Mix bedding mortar using a bagged sand-cement mortar mix to a dryish consistency. Spread it about 75mm deep in the gap.

4 Dampen the new kerbstone and lower it into position. Cushion it with a 50mm piece of flat timber and tap it down with a club hammer until it is flush with the adjoining kerbstone.

5 Use a spirit level to check that the sides align with the adjoining kerbstone, and a straightedge to check that the surface is also aligned.

Repairing cracks or holes in concrete

Hairline cracks in concrete can be ignored. They often follow the lines of the contraction joints between sections.
• A hole can be filled if it is at least 15mm deep. If the hole is shallower, deepen it first, or the new layer will be too thin to hold firm.
• Repair concrete with a filler containing PVA adhesive (see panel, above left) to make a good bond.
• For potholes, use dry ready-mixed concrete filler instead.

1 Widen the crack or hole below the surface by undercutting the edges with a cold chisel and club hammer. This ensures that the filler will be well anchored.

2 Remove all debris from the hole or crack and brush it with a priming coat of PVA adhesive as instructed on the container – usually one part adhesive to five parts water.

3 When the priming coat is tacky, fill the crack or hole using concrete filler (see panel, above left). Pack it well down so that there are no air pockets, which will weaken the concrete.

4 Level off the area flush with the surrounding surface using a brick trowel or plasterer's steel finishing trowel.

5 Keep the repair covered with polythene for at least three days.

Repairing crumbling edges on a concrete path

Concrete may crumble at the edges if the edging formwork was removed too soon, or if the wet concrete was not packed well down against the formwork during laying. Air pockets below an apparently solid surface cause the concrete to break up when the edges come under pressure during use.

1 Chip away the damaged concrete back to solid material, using a cold chisel and club hammer.

2 Remove the debris, and if the sub-base is exposed, ram the hardcore well down with a ramming tool or thick length of timber. Add fresh hardcore to any soft spots and ram it well down.

3 Set up timber edging 25mm thick alongside the damaged area so that the top edge is level with the concrete surface. Support it with pegs driven into the ground.

4 Brush the exposed edge of the concrete with a priming coat of PVA adhesive mixed according to the instructions on the container – usually one part adhesive to five parts water.

5 Prepare concrete filler (page 97) and use a bricklaying trowel to press into the exposed area, well down against the edging.

6 Level the surface with the trowel, or use a wood float, letting the concrete build up on the float face, to give a course non-slip finish.

7 Cover the repaired area with polythene to stop it drying too fast. Remove the sheeting after three days. Leave the edging longer if the path is used a lot.

Repairing a concrete step

1 Cut back a crumbling edge using a cold chisel and club hammer. If the surface is worn down, score it with a brick bolster and hammer to provide a good grip (key) for a new layer of concrete.

2 Fix timber edging round the step using pegs and bricks to keep it firmly in place. If renewing a worn surface, set the edging about 15mm higher than the surface, with the side pieces allowing a forward slope of about 10mm for water to run off.

3 Brush away dust and debris.

4 Prime the area with a mixture of PVA adhesive and water according to the container instructions – usually one part adhesive to five parts water.

5 Repair crumbling edges with concrete filler (page 97). Press it will down against the edging.

Alternatively To re-surface the step, use bagged sand-cement mix. Prepare the concrete following the instructions on the bag but first coat the surface with a solution of three parts PVA adhesive to one part water. Before it dries, apply the concrete to lie level with top of the edging.

6 Level the area. Cover for three days, as for path repairs.

Mortar and concrete basics

Cement, sand and hydrated lime mixed with water make up the mortar used to stick bricks together in walls. Concrete is used for a variety of garden features, from laying paths and patios to anchoring fence posts.

Making mortar

Use strong mortar for a garden wall, to withstand winds and rain. The standard mix is suitable for more sheltered areas. You can buy ready-mixed bags of dry bricklaying mortar to which only water has to be added. This is more expensive, but convenient for small jobs.

Mortar becomes unusable within two hours of mixing (sooner if the weather is hot). Mix it in small batches to avoid waste. After a time you will be able to gauge how much to make up at a time, according to the rate at which you can lay the bricks.

Use the following ingredient ratios to prepare a mortar mix:

Strong mix: Make this with 1 part ordinary Portland cement to ½ part hydrated lime to 4 parts builder's sand.

Standard mix: You will need 1 part ordinary Portland cement to 1 part hydrated lime to 6 parts builder's sand.

Making concrete

The ratio of cement to sand and aggregate determines how strong a concrete mix is. If you are mixing concrete yourself, order sand and aggregate combined (known as all-in aggregate).

The volume of concrete you make depends entirely on the volume of aggregate you use. The cement does not add to the final volume because the particles fill the voids between the stones and bond them together into a solid mass as the concrete sets. This means that to make one cubic meter ($1m^3$) of concrete you need $1m^3$ of all-in aggregate, plus an amount of cement that is determined by the strength of mix you are intending to make.

Use the following ingredient ratios for three standard concrete mixes:

Foundation mix This consists of 1 part cement to 5 parts all-in aggregate, equivalent to 6 bags of cement per m^3 of all-in aggregate. Use this relatively weak mix for any concrete that will be buried underground and not exposed to the weather. Typical jobs include laying a strip foundation for a wall, a base for a path that will be surfaced with another paving material, or an anchor for a fence post.

General-purpose mix Make this with 1 part cement to 4 parts all-in aggregate, equivalent to 7 bags of cement per m^3 of aggregate. Use this mix for most jobs other than foundations. Uses include a slab base for an outbuilding or garage.

Paving mix You will need 1 part cement to 3.5 parts all-in aggregate, equivalent to 8 bags of cement per m^3 of aggregate. Use this mix for concrete paths and patios, which will be left exposed to the weather.

To find the volume of concrete you need, measure the area and multiply this by the thickness needed. Always work in metric measurements, and add 10 per cent to the total volume to allow for wastage and the filling of uneven sub-bases.

Measuring and mixing mortar or concrete

1 Measure out the number of buckets of sand or aggregate you require on the mixing surface.

2 Use a separate bucket and shovel to measure out the cement and add it to the sand. Do not use the bucket and shovel for other ingredients or mixing, or the cement in the bag could get damp and be spoiled.

3 Mix the sand or all-in aggregate and cement together thoroughly with the other shovel. If you are preparing mortar, mix in the hydrated lime once the sand and cement are mixed together.

4 Make a crater at the top of the pile and pour in a little water from a watering can. Shovel from the outside of the pile into the middle to mix in the water in the crater.

5 Continue adding small amounts of water and turning the pile over with the shovel until the mortar or cement is a stiff mix that falls off the spade cleanly.

Tools you will need for building a wall

Line pins and building line The flat-bladed steel pins are pushed into the mortar joints at the end of the wall once the ends or corners have been built up. The line stretched between them is raised for each course as a levelling guide while laying bricks or blocks.

Line pins and building line

Profile boards

Plumb line Useful for checking that the wall is vertical. The line can be tied round and notched into a piece of board placed on the top course, so that it hangs down the wall as a guide while you work.

Plumb line

Profile board For marking the edges of strip foundations and walls. Make a uniform pair, or two pairs if the wall turns a corner. For each, use a board about 450–600mm long nailed across two 600mm battens with pointed ends for driving into the soil. Notch the top edge of the board at suitable distances to mark each edge of the foundation strip and wall. The notches hold guidelines stretched taut between boards, one at each end of the site. Nails can be used instead of notches.

Gauge rod Used to check that each course of bricks is the correct height. Make one from a length of 75 x 25mm timber. For brick courses, mark the gauge every 75mm. For screen block walling, mark the gauge every 200mm for pier pilasters, and every 300mm for blocks. If using other types of walling block, mark it to match the course heights (including mortar) required.

Gauge rod

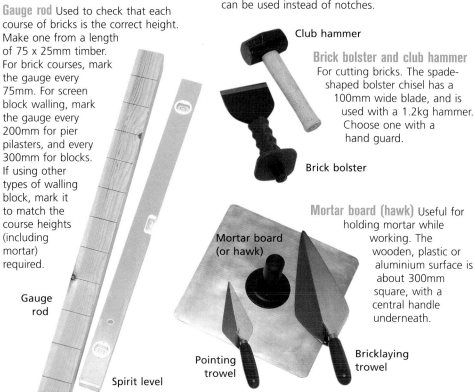

Club hammer

Brick bolster and club hammer For cutting bricks. The spade-shaped bolster chisel has a 100mm wide blade, and is used with a 1.2kg hammer. Choose one with a hand guard.

Brick bolster

Mortar board (hawk) Useful for holding mortar while working. The wooden, plastic or aluminium surface is about 300mm square, with a central handle underneath.

Mortar board (or hawk)

Pointing trowel

Bricklaying trowel

Spirit level

Pointing trowel A small trowel with a blade 75–200mm long, used for shaping mortar joints.

Spirit level Used for checking the alignment of walls. It should have both horizontal and vertical vials, and preferably be about 1m long.

Bricklaying trowel A large trowel with a blade 250–330mm long, for spreading mortar when laying bricks.

Choosing walling materials

Walls can be used to delineate boundaries, to create a terrace on a sloped area or to make a raised bed or BBQ. Your choice of material will depend not only on the look you want to achieve, but also on your budget. You must also ensure that you use the correct mortar – unless you have chosen a mortar-free option. Your supplier will be able to advise you.

Mortar-free

• Suitable for raised beds up to 6 courses only – the earth inside the bed stabilises the structure
• Easy and quick to build
• Blocks stack – if you make a mistake, you can start again
• No need for concrete footings
• Not suitable as a free-standing or dividing wall

Composite blocks

• Suitable for walls up to 1 metre high
• Each reconstituted stone block looks like several interlocking pieces making the building process fast and straightforward
• A choice of finishes including 'dry-stone walling' and 'weathered block wall'
• Some styles available in very large blocks so a large area can be built fast
• Some types use outdoor grade brick adhesive to allow easier construction
• Special curved blocks available for the creation of circles or fluid curves

Screening blocks
• Suitable for patios or perhaps carports
• Moulded blocks with a cut-out design
• Gives privacy but lets light through
• Relatively lightweight to handle
• Straightforward to build
• Built using mortar or custom adhesive
• Must be laid on concrete footings

Natural stone and traditional brick

• Suitable for walls up to 1 metre high
• Needs concrete footings and mortar
• Suitable only for experienced builders
• Natural stone is expensive
• Natural stone may vary in size and thickness: this must be allowed for in mortar
• Bricks are uniform in size and less forgiving than stone, so accurate laying is essential

COPINGS AND CAPPINGS

The top course of a wall – a single finishing layer of bricks, slabs or coordinating coping blocks or bricks – is functional as well as decorative. It ensures that water runs off the top instead of soaking in: in winter, water can freeze causing damage to the wall. Copings overhang the wall; cappings are flush.

Laying strip foundations

Every wall must be built on a firm, level foundation or it will soon crack and fall down.

Before you start The usual foundation is a solid layer of concrete on a bed of hardcore, though hardcore is not necessary if the ground beneath is firm. A low wall can be built on a flat, firm surface such as a patio, as long as it has an adequate sub-base and the slabs are set on a full bed of mortar. Set it back from the edge of the surface by the same distance as its thickness (and by a minimum of 150mm).

Tools *Spade; profile boards (page 100); string; heavy hammer; earth rammer (page 90) or stout length of timber; pencil or chalk; steel tape measure; spirit level; rake; straight-edged board; brick trowel.*

Materials *Hardcore (page 88); marker pegs 460mm long; concrete; sharp sand.*

---

1 Mark the edge of each side of the foundation strip using string lines and profile boards (see below).

2 Remove 50–75mm of topsoil and spread it elsewhere on the ground.

3 Measure from the top of each marker peg and mark lines showing the bottom of the concrete layer (page 88). Drive in marker pegs on each side of the strip at about 1m intervals, with their tops at the required height for the surface of the concrete. Generally, the concrete is level with a hard surrounding surface, or 25–50mm below a lawn edge.

4 Level adjacent and opposite pegs using a spirit level, set on a length of board.

5 Dig a trench as wide as the marked lines and to the required overall depth, using the bottom line on the marker pegs as a guide. If the soil is still soft, dig a little deeper.

6 Fill the bottom of the trench with hardcore to the height of the guideline on the marker pegs. Ram the hardcore down well using an earth rammer or a stout length of timber. Cover with a blinding layer of sharp sand, to fill any gaps.

7 Mix the concrete (see page 99) on a clean surface and shovel it into the trench. Spread it with a rake, making sure it reaches well into the corners and is level with the tops of the marker pegs. Use the edge of a straight-edged board to tamp across the concrete to expel air.

Foundation measurements

As a general guide, use a strip 150mm thick and 300mm wide for a half-brick wall up to a maximum of 1m high. Increase this to 225mm thick and 450mm wide for a one-brick wall up to 1m high, and to 300mm thick for a one-brick wall over 1m high (up to a maximum of 2m).

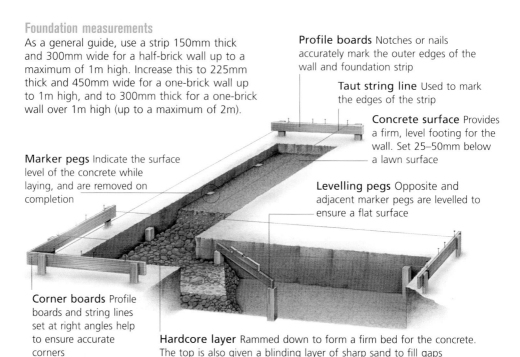

Profile boards Notches or nails accurately mark the outer edges of the wall and foundation strip

Taut string line Used to mark the edges of the strip

Concrete surface Provides a firm, level footing for the wall. Set 25–50mm below a lawn surface

Marker pegs Indicate the surface level of the concrete while laying, and are removed on completion

Levelling pegs Opposite and adjacent marker pegs are levelled to ensure a flat surface

Corner boards Profile boards and string lines set at right angles help to ensure accurate corners

Hardcore layer Rammed down to form a firm bed for the concrete. The top is also given a blinding layer of sharp sand to fill gaps

8 Remove the marker pegs and fill the gaps with concrete, smoothing the surface with the board. Leave the profile boards in position and fit string lines to mark wall edges for bricklaying.

9 Mark the positions of the string guidelines for the walls on the concrete strip. Do this either before the concrete sets (a few hours after laying) using a spirit level, or when the concrete is hard, using a chalked string line.

10 Cover the concrete with polythene sheeting and weight the edges of the sheeting with bricks to stop it blowing away. Let it cure and harden for at least three days before building on top of it.

Laying bricks or walling blocks

Take particular care in positioning and laying the first course – it is the most crucial part of the job.

Before you start Work out the bond pattern using dry bricks, especially if the wall has any corners or piers (page 106), before laying any bricks or walling blocks on the strip foundation. Make a note of how many part bricks you will need to cut (page 105). Use special-quality frost-resistant bricks either for the whole wall or at least for the first two courses. For an ordinary (M grade) brick wall, use a damp-proof membrane under the coping.

It takes experience to achieve a 10mm thickness of mortar under a brick every time. If you have never done any bricklaying before, practise laying a few bricks with a pseudo mortar of one part lime and three parts sand. Clean the bricks within two hours so that they can be used again. Discard the mortar.

Tools *Brick trowel; spirit level; flat, even length of timber; builder's square; gauge rod with 75mm markings; pointing trowel; line pins and building line; mortar board; jointing tools; straightedge.*

Materials *Bricks or walling blocks; coping or capping bricks; strong mortar (page 101); damp-proof membrane about 20mm narrower than the wall thickness.*

1 Leave the profile boards and string lines in position as a guide until you have completed the first course.

2 Shape the mortar with the trowel so that it looks like a fat sausage pointed at both ends.

3 Slide the trowel underneath the mortar to lift it up.

4 Tip the mortar onto the building surface between the marked lines (facing page) in position for laying the first brick.

5 Tap the flat of the trowel blade backwards along the mortar to flatten it to a thickness of about 20mm. The mortar will be pressed down to 10mm thick by the weight of the brick.

6 Lay the first brick in position on the mortar in line with the marked guidelines. If the brick has a frog (indentation on one side) lay it with the frog facing upwards.

7 Lay another brick in the same way a few feet farther along the line. Do not worry about its position in the bond, it is for levelling only and can be removed later.

8 Place a flat board across the tops of the two bricks and use a spirit level to check that it is horizontal. Use the trowel handle to tap down the higher of the two bricks as necessary until both bricks are level.

9 Prepare a mortar bed for the second brick of the course. Before laying the brick, hold it upright and spread mortar for the vertical joint on the end to be butted. Squash the mortar down against all four edges, or it will easily slip off. Lift the levelling brick out of the way.

10 Lay the next four or five bricks of the course in the same way, then place a spirit level along them to check that they are horizontal. Tap bricks down with a trowel handle as necessary. If a brick is too low, remove it and add more mortar.

11 If the course turns a right-angled corner, use a builder's square to make sure it is true.

12 After completing the first course, build up at each end and corner with three or four stepped courses. Use the gauge rod to check that each course is at the correct height.

13 Insert line pins into the mortar at each built-up end. Use the line between them as a guide to levelling the top of the second course. Move it up progressively to check the levels of following courses as you lay the bricks between the stepped ends.

14 Point the joints after laying three or four courses (see right).

Building a freestanding wall

Strip foundation Concrete thickness as required (see opposite)

Builder's square for checking that right-angled corners are true

Profile board Used to stretch string lines for marking edges of strip foundation and position marks for wall edges

Gauge rod For checking that each course is the correct height

Position marks Lines marked to show the wall edges, as a guide to laying the first brick course

Spirit level Use the vertical vial to make sure the wall is upright. Use horizontally to make sure the wall surface is straight

Line pins and building line A line stretched between line pins stuck in the mortar at each end, as a guide for levelling each course

Weather protection Two bottom courses or special quality bricks such as Class B engineering bricks or frost-resistant (F grade) bricks

Stepped end End bricks of the first three or four courses built up in steps before each complete course is laid

15 From time to time check that the wall is both upright and straight by using a spirit level against it vertically and horizontally.

16 If using a top course of shaped bricks, sandwich the damp-proof membrane into the mortar two courses from the top. If using coping stones, sandwich it into the mortar bed for the coping.

Cutting a brick

Cutting a brick in half lengthways (called a closer) is tricky, as the brick is likely to fracture. It is generally easier to cut two quarter bricks from a half brick and lay them end on instead of using a closer. The easiest way is with a brick bolster and club hammer.

1 Mark the cutting line round the brick, then score along it with the bolster, tapping it gently with a club hammer.

2 With the brick laid frog down on sand or grass, rest the bolster in the scored line with its handle tilted slightly towards the waste end of the brick. Then strike it hard with the club hammer. The brick should break neatly in two.

Cutting a block A solid walling block can also be cut with a bolster and hammer. Mark the cutting line and continuously score round it, gradually increasing pressure until it breaks in two. As an alternative, you can use a block splitter (page 95).

Using an angle grinder If you have a lot of bricks to cut, hire an angle grinder, but handle it with care to avoid an accident.
Wear safety goggles and heavy gloves as protection from flying fragments.

Pointing the joints

Mortar joints between bricks are shaped so that they shed rainwater and look neat. The commonest shapes used are flush, concave, and weatherstruck (sloped outwards from a recess at the top of the joint).

The shaping, generally known as pointing, can be done after each course before the mortar dries, or left until later using fresh mortar – of a different colour if desired. If pointing is to be left until later, when you have laid a few courses, rake out some of the mortar from each joint to leave a 15mm deep recess.

Flush joint Made by trimming off excess mortar with a pointing trowel so that it is in line with the adjoining bricks. Rub the joint smooth with a piece of sacking.

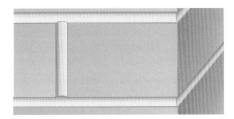

Concave joint Made by trimming off the excess mortar with a trowel, then drawing a rounded piece of metal along the joint to give it an inward curve. You can use a bent piece of 15mm copper pipe or a piece of garden hosepipe.

Weatherstruck joint Made by using the pointing trowel to recess the mortar slightly below the upper brick, and then sloping it to project slightly above the lower brick.
Trim off the mortar from the overhang at the base using a straightedge and the trowel. Shape the vertical joints in the same way, but all sloped in the same direction.

Building a brick pier

A pier is not only decorative in a brick wall, but it also adds stability. There are four basic types of pier, but the inventive bricklayer may find more.

End pier on half-brick wall

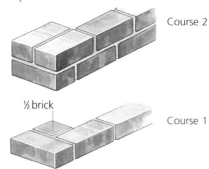

Course 2

½ brick

Course 1

A half-brick (stretcher bond) wall is 103mm thick. To make an end pier projecting on one side only, lay a header brick against the end stretcher on the first course, then a half brick in the angle between header and stretcher.

On the second course of the pier, lay two stretcher bricks, then continue the course by laying more stretchers.

Intermediate pier on half-brick wall

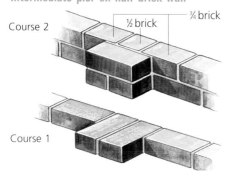

Course 2   ¾ brick
½ brick

Course 1

For the first course of an intermediate pier projecting on one side only, lay two header bricks to project from the bond in the place of one of the stretchers at the required positions – usually at 1.8m intervals.

On the second course, the projecting headers are covered with a stretcher, and at the inner end are overlapped by stretchers. To avoid a constant vertical joint on the wall face, use two three-quarter bricks with a half brick in between.

End pier on full-brick wall

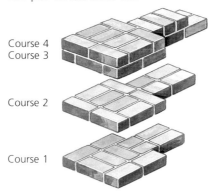

Course 4
Course 3

Course 2

Course 1

For an end pier on a full-brick wall built with an English garden wall bond, end the course with two three-quarter bricks. Then lay three headers at the end of the wall. Place two head-on stretchers on each side so that the pier projects half a brick on each side, and runs half a brick beside the three-quarter bricks.

End the second course with three-quarter bricks, then butt headers across the pier at each end, with four parallel stretchers between. Repeat the pattern for alternate courses. On the fourth (header) course, no three-quarter bricks will be needed because this course is all headers.

Intermediate double pier on full-brick wall

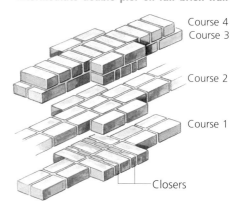

Course 4
Course 3

Course 2

Course 1

Closers

For an intermediate pier projecting from both sides of a wall built with an English garden wall bond, interrupt the first stretcher course with three pairs of head-on headers with two pairs of head-on closers between them. This will project half a brick on each side of the wall.

For the second course, lay two head-on stretchers on each side on the projecting half bricks. Repeat the pattern for alternate courses. The only variation is that on the fourth (header) course the pier stretchers are alongside headers.

Building a brick retaining wall

A retaining wall supports a bank of earth on one side, and may be needed in a sloping garden, or as a base for a boundary fence where the neighbouring garden is at a higher level.

Before you start Your retaining wall can be built of bricks or walling blocks in the usual way, but must be a full-brick wall – about 215mm thick – built with a strong bond and strong mortar (page 99). If the ground behind the wall either slopes upwards or seems unstable, or if you want to build a wall higher than 1m, get the advice of a consulting engineer.

The strip foundations (page 102) should be set in a trench with the top of the concrete surface about 250mm below the level of the lower ground, so that the bottom of the front of the wall is a little below ground level.

To allow for drainage from the banked soil, make drain holes through the wall. One way is to leave out the mortar in every other vertical joint in the second course above the lower ground level. This is simplest to do between headers. Another way is to angle plastic or clay pipes through the wall at 1m intervals.

Making movement joints

In a long run of wall, a movement joint is needed to allow for shrinkage or expansion of the materials. The joint is a narrow vertical gap about 10mm wide in the wall and coping, completely separating one length of wall from the next.

Make movement joints at the intervals recommended for the type of wall you are building. Flemish bond walls require movement joints every 8m for clay bricks, and every 4m for blocks or calcium-silicate bricks. This is the most common method and is recommended for stretcher, English garden wall and open or honeycomb patterns. However, random pattern walls should have them no farther apart than every 4m.

Once the wall is complete, fill the gaps with strips of plastic foam and seal them on each side with a generous bead of non-setting exterior-quality mastic.

A brick retaining wall
To last for years and be sturdy and safe, a brick retaining wall needs sound foundations, two or three courses of frost-resistant bricks, good drainage and well-spaced movement joints (above). Check retaining walls regularly, as even a small wall can cause damage or injury should it collapse.

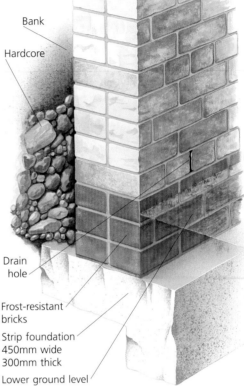

Bank

Hardcore

Drain hole

Frost-resistant bricks

Strip foundation 450mm wide 300mm thick

Lower ground level

Building steps into a slope

Roughly shape the slope before you start building the steps. If it is steep, remove some of the soil. On an irregular slope, build up with soil from other parts of the garden.

The layout of the slope may suggest two flights of steps at right angles, with a landing in between. On a long flight, make a landing after about every ten steps to provide a resting place. On flights with high, loose soil at the sides, you will need to build low brick retaining walls (above).

The instructions given here are for steps built with brick risers and concrete paving slab treads, but the method is similar whatever material you use.

Steps should be evenly spaced and not less than 600mm wide. For two people to walk comfortably abreast, the width must be at least 1.5m. Use the guidelines below to work out the dimensions.

Working out step dimensions

To decide on the number of treads and risers for a flight of steps, measure the following:
• The height difference between the two levels.
• The length of the slope.

For each measurement, calculate the number of steps needed for various combinations of treads and risers until you get more or less the same number for both measurements. For example, for a slope 1.8m long with a 600mm difference in height, follow these steps.

1 Choose a suitable riser height and divide it into the height difference. As the slope is gentle, choose a low riser:
Height difference 600mm divided by 100mm riser = 6 steps.

2 The best tread for a 100mm riser is 460mm. Divide this into the slope length:
Slope length 1.8m ÷ 460mm tread = 4 steps.

Steps built into a slope The ground is roughly shaped for the treads and risers. The first riser is built on a footing strip, and each following riser on the back of the previous tread. Treads are bedded on hardcore with a built-in drainage slope.

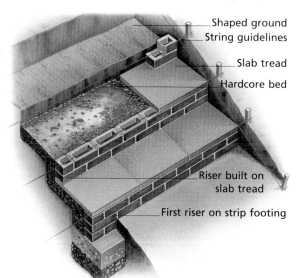

Shaped ground
String guidelines
Slab tread
Hardcore bed
Riser built on slab tread
First riser on strip footing

3 To adjust the difference, try again with a higher riser and a shorter tread:
Height 600mm ÷ 120mm = 5
Length 1.8m ÷ 400mm = 4.5
So 5 steps will fit comfortably.

Tools *String and pegs; 5m steel tape measure; long length of timber; spirit level; builder's square; spade; club hammer; brick trowel; mortar mixing board; two heavy-duty polythene buckets and two shovels (for mixing concrete); short tamping beam; pointing trowel or joining tool; earth rammer; 10mm thick wooden batten. Possibly also a brick bolster.*

Materials *Hardcore – one barrowload fills about 0.5m² at 150mm deep; concrete foundation mix; bricks; bricklaying mortar (page 99); paving slabs; bedding mortar; water. Possibly also sharp sand.*

1 Fix two parallel string lines from top to bottom of the slope, as far apart as the required step width.

2 Measure a line to find the length of the slope.

3 To measure the height difference between the levels, rest one end of a length of timber on the top of the slope and place a spirit level on it. Get a helper to hold the timber level while you measure the height of the timber above the lower ground level.

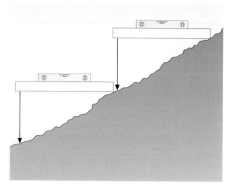

Alternatively If the timber will not reach the whole way, measure to a point halfway down the slope, then measure from the same point to the lowest level. Add the two heights together for the total fall.

4 Calculate a suitable dimension for treads and risers (see above).

5 Fix string lines to mark the front edge of each step. Make sure they are evenly spaced, and use a builder's square to check that they are at right angles to the length lines.

6 Use a spade to shape the ground for each step. Begin at the bottom so you always have a flat area to work from.

7 Dig a trench 125mm deep at the base of the flight to make a footing strip for the first riser.

8 Tip about 25mm of hardcore into the base of the trench and ram it well down.

11 Wait at least two hours for the mortar to dry before ramming down a layer of hardcore for the first tread behind the riser. Take care not to disturb the bricks and fresh mortar. Slope the hardcore surface to the front for drainage (see page 110).

12 Lay paving slabs to make the surface of the first tread. Use a full bed of mortar and project the slab about 25mm in front of the riser.

9 Fill the trench with concrete, tamp level with the ground and cover it with polythene sheet.

10 Wait three days before building the first riser on the footing strip (see Laying bricks, page 103).

13 Build the next riser on the back edge of the first tread. Make sure the riser is vertical – use the mortar layer to adjust for the slight drainage slope on the tread.

14 Make sure the top tread is level with the surrounding ground. If necessary, slope the ground towards the tread, or raise the tread slightly – no more than 15mm.

15 Fill in between the tread slabs with mortar or sharp sand. If you use mortar, wait about 24 hours before using the steps, to allow the mortar to set.

Sloping a tread for drainage

1 Build up the hardcore surface a little higher at the back of the step. Slope the surface to level with the top of the riser at the front.

2 To check the slope, lay a spirit level from the back to the front with a 10mm thick wooden batten under the front edge, on the riser. Build up the back of the slope until the spirit level is horizontal with the wooden batten in place.

3 Check that the hardcore area is level from side to side.

Making a raised brick bed

A hollow bed for planting is simply a wall that completely encloses a small area filled with soil.

Build a brick wall 215mm thick (page 103), either on a strip foundation surrounding an area of soil, or on a solid surface such as a patio. A useful height for a raised bed is 500mm. If it is any higher, the pressure of the soil as the weather causes it to expand or shrink could force the walls outwards. Do not make the bed wider than about 1m. Not only will it take a lot of soil to fill it, but it will be difficult to reach plants in the centre.

Tools *Brick trowel; spirit level.*

Materials *Bricks or walling blocks; mortar (page 99).*

1 Mark out the area and calculate how many bricks you need; allow four and a half bricks per metre per course (four per yard). Lay the first course of bricks on a thin layer of stiffish mortar spread on the paving.

2 As you work, keep checking levels with a spirit level. Adjust the thickness of the mortar to compensate for a very slight fall. Leave gaps between bricks at intervals to allow excess water to drain out.

3 When you lay the second course, place the corner brick endways on, in order to make a strong bond.

4 Lay the top course of bricks upside down, so the top is flush. Leave for two days until the mortar has set hard. Then fill with soil, using a good quality, free-draining loam or a mixture of loam and peat.

Building a barbecue

A built-in barbecue gives you a custom-made cooking area designed to fit your garden. Think long and hard about the right size, the best site and the most suitable design.

The dimensions of a barbecue are dictated by the size of the grill and the charcoal pan. So purchase these first, or buy a built-in barbecue kit to use as a template.

Try to site a barbecue on or near the patio. For convenience it should also be fairly close to the kitchen. Pick a spot that is out of direct view of the house windows, if possible, unless you want to look at the barbecue all the year round, and avoid having any potential fire hazards nearby, such as fences, trellis or pergolas.

Tools *Spirit level; builder's square; stick of chalk; brick trowel; plumb line.*

Materials *Bricks sufficient for ten courses; dry-mix mortar; grill and charcoal pan, or a built-in barbecue kit.*

Before you start A firm, level base is essential. If a suitable area of concrete, slabs or brick is not available, lay a concrete foundation before you begin to build.

1 Use the spirit level to check the ground is level. Without mortar, lay out the first course of bricks in a double L shape. With the builder's square, check the corners are exact right angles and ensure that the charcoal pan will fit correctly. Draw around the bricks with chalk, then move them out of the way.

2 Mix the mortar and, using a brick trowel, put a layer of mortar on the ground. Place the first course of bricks on top. Use the builder's square to check the corners are still at right angles, and ensure the bricks are level.

3 Place a layer of mortar on top of the bricks and lay the second course of bricks so that the joints are staggered. Continue to lay courses of bricks in this way, frequently checking for level. Check that the walls are level using a plumb line.

4 Once you reach the height convenient for the charcoal pan (about six courses), lay three bricks so they stick out at right angles on each side. These bricks will support the charcoal pan. Lay a further one or two courses of bricks, then repeat the right-angled bricks to provide support for the grill. If you wish to vary the grill height, set short metal bars in the mortar between two or more courses of bricks.

5 Add a further one or two courses of bricks above the highest grill setting. If the barbecue is in an exposed position, you could raise the top by two or three more courses to create a partial windbreak.

Installing a flexible pond liner

Making a pond with a flexible liner simply involves digging a hole and placing the liner inside, so that the size and shape of the pond can be to your own design.

Tools *Garden hosepipe; spade; spirit level; straight-edged plank; scissors; sand for marking out the area; bricks to use as temporary weights.*

Materials *Flexible liner; protective underlay of the same size as the liner; edging materials such as rocks, pebbles, coarse gravel, paving slabs; turf.*

Calculating the size of the liner

To find the area of liner required, multiply the length by the width as follows:
Length = maximum overall length
+ (2 x maximum depth) + 300mm
Width = maximum overall width
+ (2 x maximum depth) + 300mm
This formula works for all ponds regardless of shape and size. The extra 300mm is to allow for adequate overlap around the edges of the pond.

CHOOSING A LINER

Flexible liners are available in a range of materials from PVC to butyl rubber. Buy the best you can afford, because cheaper materials have a shorter life. The length of guarantee is a guide to a good liner; the best quality materials will be guaranteed for at least 20 years. Liners come in rolls of varying width – take this into account when planning the dimensions of the pond.

1 Mark out the shape of the pond using a hosepipe. View it from every angle including from an upstairs window. When you are completely happy with the shape and the overall position of the pond, trickle sand onto the ground to mark the outline, then remove the hosepipe.

2 Dig out the pond cavity just inside the sand mark. Make the sides slope outwards by at least 20° to stop the soil crumbling into the hole. Shape underwater shelves around the edge 300mm deep and 250–300mm wide. Outside the sand mark, remove a 450mm strip of soil or turf to a depth of 50mm to accommodate the overlap around the pond edges.

3 Use a spirit level placed on a plank to check that the rim of the pool is level all the way round, as any discrepancies will show up dramatically when the pond is full of water. If you plan to have a bog garden next to the pond, make the adjoining edge 50mm lower than the rest of the rim. Check that the underwater shelves are level, too.

4 Once digging is complete, check over the entire cavity and remove any debris and protruding stones that could damage the liner. Firm the sides with your hands to remove any soft spots that could subside later on. Line the cavity with protective underlay.

5 Cut the pond liner to size, if necessary. Lay it loosely over the cavity and weigh down the edges temporarily with bricks. When handling the liner, take care that it does not catch on any sharp objects. This part of the job is best done by two people with plenty of time to get things right.

6 Start running in water from a hose once the liner is centred over the hole. The increasing weight of the water will mould the liner to the shape of the cavity. As the liner sinks, move the weights and fold the liner neatly around shelves and corners. Continue filling the pond until the water is just below the rim.

7 Trim the liner to leave an overlap of 150mm all round. Bury the outside edge of the liner in the soil, leaving a rim of exposed liner 50–100mm wide.

8 Edge the pond with materials to conceal the liner rim. Let paving stones project over the water by 50mm to conceal the liner; turf should butt up to the edge.

Installing a rigid pond liner

Rigid liners are made of reinforced plastic. The hole you dig needs to be an accurate match for the shape of the pond: the simpler the shape, the easier this is to achieve.

Symmetrical, geometrically shaped liners are relatively easy to install (see below). A rigid liner or mould of an asymmetric shape, however, must be stood upright in position to mark out its form, or you will get a mirror image. Prop the liner upright, sticking canes in the ground to hold it in place and indicate its outline, before excavating the soil.

Tools *Spade; spirit level; straight-edged plank.*

Materials *Rigid liner; sand for marking out; hardcore or crushed stone; materials for edging, such as paving slabs. Possibly also coarse sand.*

1 Mark out the shape of the pond. Lay the liner upside down on the site and, using sand, trace the outline of the liner onto the ground. Remove the liner.

2 Cut the outline of the pond into the soil using a sharp spade to ensure straight lines.

3 Dig out the pond cavity just inside the cut lines, but only as deep as the shallow marginal shelf. Check across the edges using a spirit level and straight-edged plank to ensure that they are level.

4 Place the liner in the hole the right way up and mark around the base of the deepest part of the pond with sand. Remove the liner.

5 Cut the outline for the deep part of the pond in the soil, then dig out the hole to the correct depth. Clear away all loose stones and roots. On stony soil, make the hole a bit deeper, and place a 50mm layer of coarse sand on which the liner can rest.

6 Check that the liner fits in the hole, and dig out more soil if necessary. Ensure the liner is level in each direction by placing the spirit level along each edge. Make any necessary adjustments and back-fill with soil or sand.

7 Slowly fill the liner with water, allowing the mould to settle under its increasing weight. Check for level as it fills and adjust the liner as necessary, otherwise one edge will stand above the water line and be unsightly.

8 As the liner is filling up, back-fill the gaps with soil or sand. When it is level, prepare the ground for paving around the liner, if you are having paved edges. Place a 100mm layer of hardcore or crushed stone and ram down with a post to compact it.

9 Bed each paving slab onto the hardcore, overhanging the edge of the liner slightly. Tap each one into position and check for level before mortaring the gaps.

Installing a pebble fountain

Most garden centres now sell pebble or bubble fountain kits, consisting of a plastic bucket with a lid and a wide collar. You will also need a pond pump and a decorative disguise for the surface.

SAFETY TIP

Mixing electricity with water and the outdoors can be dangerous. If you are installing a water feature that requires a mains power supply, follow the instructions for wiring outdoor electrics on pages 118–122 and always connect the water pump to an RCD.

5 Connect the pump to the power supply via a low-voltage transformer inside the house. Switch on the fountain to check that it is working. If you are not confident about wiring in the pump, call in an electrician. Mains outdoor electrics should always be connected via a residual current device (RCD) and installed with great care.

1 Start by digging a hole to take the bucket. Position the bucket in the hole.

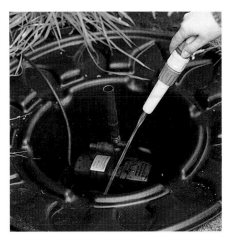

6 Fill the reservoir with water and test the pump. You may need to adjust the flow rate or positioning to achieve the effect you want.

7 When you are happy, fit the lid and cover the top with your chosen decoration.

2 The lip of the plastic collar should be flush with the surrounding earth. Using a spirit level check that the feature is level all the way round.

3 Line the hole with soft sand to prevent sharp stones from puncturing the plastic.

4 Put the pond in place, position your pump in the base and run the electric cable away, hiding it among surrounding plants. You could protect the cable in a length of metal conduit.

8 Pebbles, gravel and large cobbles work well with a bubbling stream of water. You could run a hose from the pump through a glazed terracotta ball with a hole drilled in the top. Or fit the pump with a spray attachment and hide it with pots of plants that are happy being splashed with water.

Installing a wall-mounted water fountain

Running water adds a magical touch to any garden. The installation techniques shown here can be used for rills, water chutes and many more water features.

Tools *Spirit level; power drill and masonry bit; masonry paintbrush.*

Materials *20–23 litre plastic water tank (available from builders' or plumbers' merchants); length of rigid tubing; flexible piping; pump; low-voltage transformer; wall-mounted spout; wall plug and screw; bricks or slabs to disguise tank; external waterproof paint.*

1 Lift a paving slab next to a wall and dig down to create a hole big enough for the water tank, so that it sits proud of the surrounding surface by an equal amount all the way round. Make sure that the tank sits level in the hole.

2 Surround the tank with a row of bricks or walling blocks to disguise its edge. Butt the bricks tightly together, mortaring them in place if you prefer.

3 Drill a hole in the wall and insert a wall plug and screw to hold the water spout. Hang the spout in place and check with a spirit level that it is level.

4 Attach the flexible piping to the base of the spout and feed the other end into the water tank. Connect it to the pump in the base of the tank.

5 Fill the tank with water and connect the pump to the power supply via a low-voltage transformer inside the house. Switch on the fountain to check that it is working. If it is, cut the flexible piping to length so that it runs vertically into the water tank.

6 Paint the rigid tubing, which will enclose the flexible piping, to match the wall behind it. Feed the flexible pipe through the rigid tube and attach it to the pump and water spout at either end.

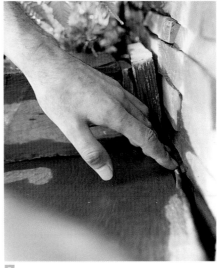

7 Tuck the electric cable running from the pump to the electricity supply along the back of the patio paving, or protect it in a length of metal conduit.

8 Fill the water tank with enough water to cover the pump, connect the power supply and switch on the pump. Add a water-loving plant, such as a fern, with its pot raised above the level of the water to complete the display.

IDEAS FOR WATER FEATURES

• You can hide the workings of a wall-mounted water feature by chasing the pipework into an existing wall or by burying the pipes in a new wall.

• A pump can also be used to move water along a shallow rill or garden stream. Dig a gently sloping trench for the rill and bury a water reservoir and pump at one end. Run a length of piping from the far end of the feature back to the reservoir to recycle the water.

Choosing garden lighting

Outdoor lighting serves several purposes. It makes it easier to find your way to, and unlock, the front door after dark; it is a deterrent to intruders; and it makes the garden a tempting proposition on a warm summer evening. In the past, outdoor lighting meant high wattage halogen security lights or garden spotlights; today's products enable you to achieve subtle effects that don't floodlight the whole garden.

LED patio lights
LED lights provide low-level lighting and add style to the garden. They can change the mood of your garden with a flick of a switch – or a remote control.
• Ideal for paths, patios, decking and steps
• Simple to fit
• Choice of colours including models that change colour
• Low energy and running costs
• Last for years
• Make hazards such as garden steps visible at night
• Some versions suitable for driveways

Low-voltage garden lights
One major avantage of low-voltage lighting is that the risk of electric shock is minimal. This makes it ideal for use outdoors. Low-voltage cables can be laid on the surface and hidden in the undergrowth.
• Suitable throughout garden
• Lights on spikes can be placed among foliage or along paths
• Submersible and floating lights available for ponds (see below)
• Net lights can liven up a garden for a party or at Christmas
• Low-voltage (12 or 24 volt) cable poses no danger and can be laid on or just below the surface

Wiring regulations

The introduction of a new section of the Building Regulations (Part P: Electrical Safety) in 2005 means that any mains wiring work out of doors now requires official approval. You can still do the work yourself, but you must notify your local authority's Building Control department of your intentions before you start the work, and pay a fee to have it inspected, tested and certificated when you have finished. Alternatively, you can employ an electrician, who must be registered with an accredited electrical self-certification scheme.

Outdoor mains lighting
Mains lighting comes in many forms, from wall lights and lamp posts to strings of weatherproof fairy lights or electric lights set in plant pots (see above).
• Suitable for most garden applications
• Cabling must be armoured or protected by PVC conduit and sunk at least 450mm deep below a driveway or 750mm in soft ground
• Circuit must be protected with an RCD
• Seek advice of a qualified electrician

Security lights
These have an infra-red sensor which activates the light when anyone comes within field of vision.
• Suitable to fit to house wall at front or back
• Can be set to stay on for a set time
• The field of activation can be adjusted
• A passive infra-red unit can activate one or several lights
• Inexpensive to buy

Fitting an outdoor wall light

One of the simplest outdoor wiring jobs is installing an outside light on the house wall. It could be a porch light by the front door, or a lantern to illuminate the patio.

Planning the route

Decide where to position the light, so you can plan the cable route to it, and work out whether it is more convenient to connect the spur to an existing lighting circuit or to a socket outlet circuit. If you want to use a lighting circuit (see Option 1, page 120), check the wattage of the new fitting; a powerful floodlight with a 250 or 500W lamp could overload an existing circuit, and is better supplied by a power circuit spur (see Option 2, page 121).

Examine the light fitting you have chosen. The simplest type is the standard bulkhead light, where you feed the supply cable in through a hole in the baseplate and connect its cores direct to the lampholder. With most other decorative outdoor light fittings, short flex tails are already connected to the lampholder and you have to connect these to the supply cable using small terminal blocks. There will usually be room within the lamp baseplate to house these blocks when you screw the lamp to the house wall.

Drilling a hole in the exterior wall

The supply cable needs to pass through the house wall immediately behind the light position. Indoors, it will either run up the wall to reach the lighting circuit in the ceiling void above, or down to reach the ground floor socket outlet circuit. To drill the hole, you will need a masonry drill bit long enough to penetrate the wall and large enough to allow you to feed the cable through the hole without chafing – typically a 10mm bit 300 or 400mm long. Drill the hole so it slopes slightly down towards the outside.

Outside work

1 Feed the end of some 1mm² two-core-and-earth cable through the hole from indoors, so about 150mm of cable projects from the wall. Remove about 75mm of the outer sheath and strip off about 12mm of the live and neutral core insulation. Cover all but 12mm of the bare earth core with green-and-yellow PVC earth sleeving.

2 Connect the cable cores to the light fitting – directly to the lampholder if it is accessible.

Alternatively Connect it to the flex tails using three terminal blocks. Connect the live cable core to the brown flex tail, the neutral core to the blue flex tail and the earth core to the green-and-yellow tail. Tighten all the terminal screws fully, then wrap the blocks tightly with PVC insulating tape.

3 Draw the cable back through the wall so you can hold the fitting against it and mark the positions of its fixing screws. Pull it away again so you can drill and plug the holes, then screw the fitting to the wall. Seal all round its baseplate with silicone mastic to keep rainwater out.

Work inside the house

Choose one of the two options below, depending on how you plan to connect up the light's power supply (see page 119).

OPTION 1 Wiring to a lighting circuit

You will need to gain access to the ceiling void by lifting floorboards so you can locate the circuit cable.

1 With the power off, cut the cable and prepare the cut ends for reconnection to a four-terminal junction box.

2 Run the cable from the outside light up the wall and into the ceiling void to reach the junction box position. Run another length of cable from the junction box to a point above where you want the switch controlling the new light, and run it down the wall to the new switch position.

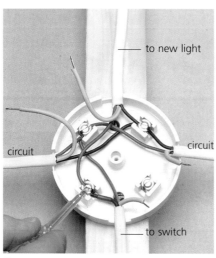

circuit

circuit

to new light

to switch

3 Screw the junction box to the joist and connect the four cables to the terminals as shown. Wrap the neutral core of the switch cable with brown PVC insulating tape to indicate that it is a live core. Screw the cover onto the junction box.

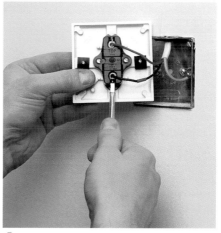

4 At the new switch position, connect the live and neutral switch cable cores to the two switch terminals and connect the sleeved earth core to the terminal in the mounting box. Again wrap the neutral core in brown PVC tape.

5 If you want to have both indoor and outdoor control of the new light, create a two-way switching arrangement (see photograph above) using two two-way switches, which have three terminals on the back of the faceplate. Run three-core-and-earth cable from the indoor switch through the wall to the outdoor one. Connect the cores at the indoor switch as shown here. At the outdoor switch, which should be a weatherproof type, connect the cores of the three-core-and-earth cable to the same terminals as in the indoor switch – brown to the terminal marked C, grey to L1 and black to L2.

6 Restore the power supply to the lighting circuit and test the new light and switching arrangement.

Wiring outdoors

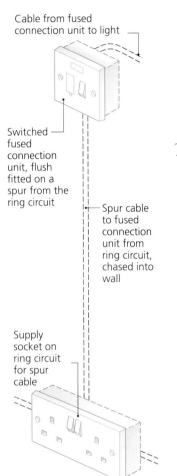

Cable from fused connection unit to light

Switched fused connection unit, flush fitted on a spur from the ring circuit

Spur cable to fused connection unit from ring circuit, chased into wall

Supply socket on ring circuit for spur cable

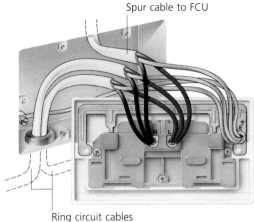

Spur cable to FCU

Ring circuit cables

Connecting at the supply socket

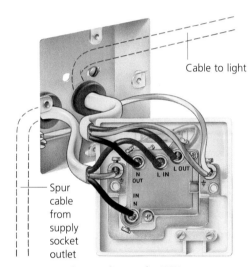

Cable to light

Spur cable from supply socket outlet

Connecting at the FCU

OPTION 2 Wiring to a spur

1 Locate a convenient socket outlet at which to make the connection, and turn the power supply to the circuit off. The spur cable will run to a switched fused connection unit (FCU) which will act as the new light switch (see diagram, above), so plan the switch position and cable runs carefully.

2 Connect a length of 2.5mm² two-core-and-earth cable into the chosen socket outlet, connecting like cores to like terminals (see Connecting at the supply socket, above). Replace the socket faceplate.

3 Run the cable to the FCU position, and connect it to the terminals marked IN or FEED. Run the 1mm² cable from the new light fitting to the FCU, and connect its cores to the terminals marked OUT or LOAD (see Connecting at the FCU diagram, above). Screw the FCU faceplate to its mounting box, and fit a 3-amp fuse in the fuseholder.

4 Restore the power supply to the circuit and test the new light and switching arrangement.

Fitting an outdoor socket

Using power tools in the garden doesn't have to mean trailing extension leads out of a window. Run a spur from an indoor power circuit and install a weatherproof outdoor socket with a high-sensitivity RCD (residual current device) that will cut out if an electrical problem occurs.

1 A neat way to fit an outdoor socket is to drill through the back of an existing indoor outlet and locate the new one on the other side of the wall.

Alternatively, run a cable along the inside wall and drill through to the outside where you want the new socket.

2 Turn off the mains power and remove the faceplate and mounting box of the socket you will be working from. Drill a pilot hole then switch to a 10mm masonry bit at least 300mm long to drill through the wall. With the power switched off, you will need a cordless drill with a hammer action, to get through the wall.

SAFETY TIP

Test the RCD before you start work every time you use your outdoor outlet. Plug in the tool, switch on and press the TEST button. If the RCD trips off, press RESET: the outlet is ready to use. If it does not, there is a fault, and you should call an electrician.

3 Screw back the mounting box and feed the new cable through the wall. Connect the old and new cores to the faceplate. There will be three cores in each terminal: the ring main cores coming in and going out, and the new spur. Reconnect the 'flying earth' cable to the box and replace the faceplate.

4 For safety, use an outside socket with an entry point through the back. Any exposed cable on an outdoor wall should be armoured or protected in a conduit. Use the grommet supplied to make the cable hole watertight, drill out any drainage holes indicated and screw the box to the wall.

5 Cover the bare earth core with PVC sleeving and connect the cores to the terminals on the faceplate. There is no need to earth a plastic mounting box. Screw the faceplate to the box. Restore the power and test both sockets before use.

Ten ways to keep your property safe

Most break-ins are carried out by casual thieves looking for easy pickings. A thief is unlikely to persist if he encounters locked doors and windows. Rapid entry and exit are vital for him, and he will not climb in and out of the house through broken glass. The tips given here will all help to keep your home secure.

1 Deliveries Cancel milk and newspapers when you go away. Arrange for a neighbour to push in unexpected items like leaflets and free newspapers. If you have a glazed porch, ask your neighbour to gather up the post each morning so that it is not visible from outside.

2 Garage Add extra security to a back door inside a garage where an intruder could work totally hidden. Ensure that the garage itself is fitted with secure locks. An electronically operated, metal up-and-over door will provide the most security.

3 Ladders Keep ladders locked away. If they must be stored outside, padlock them to a wall with special brackets.

4 Sheds If you keep valuable equipment or tools in a shed, make sure it is securely padlocked. Tools stored there could be used for a break-in. A garden spade, for example, makes a powerful lever for opening windows and a ladder can be used to access windows above the ground floor. Fit a high-security padlock and secure the hasp with nuts and bolts passing through the door and frame. Replace glass with hard-to-break polycarbonate sheet, and fit window locks to opening windows – or simply screw them shut from inside.

5 Security lights Outside lights that switch on automatically when a sensor picks up movement outside the house can be a real deterrent to crime (see page 118). Site them in areas of the house where a burglar may try to gain access, for example high above French windows at the back or over a garage door. One fitted above a front door will also help you to see who is calling at night. Site the sensor well out of reach of intruders. Bear in mind that most domestic situations do not require high power floodlights, which can be a real nuisance to neighbours.

6 Marking valuables

Print your house number and post code on valuable possessions with an ultra-violet marking pen. This will help police to prove they were stolen, and assist in returning them. Metal items can be marked with hammer-and-letter punches. Photograph valuable items together, showing on the photograph where they are marked.

7 Accessible windows Never leave windows open when you go out. Fitting security shutters will increase the safety of your property, obscuring the view inside and preventing access even if the window is broken.

Fit locks to all windows, especially those with easy access – near flat roofs, drainpipes and trees. Before buying window locks, make sure they are suitable for your windows. Make sure the frames are thick enough to accommodate the device. Most manufacturers of security devices do not recommend them for plastic windows because a thin plastic section offers no grip for screws. If you have plastic windows, consult the installer of your windows to find out which devices you can use.

Fitting laminated glass in windows can greatly add to the security. It consists of a sandwich of glass with a clear plastic film between. Although the glass may be cracked by a blow, the plastic will resist efforts to break through. Do not used wired glass because it has little security value.

SAFETY WARNING

• When windows are locked, keep a key in the room so a window can be opened in an emergency (but out of the reach of a burglar who may have smashed the glass).
• Do not permanently screw windows closed that may be needed as an escape route in time of fire.

8 Driveways

A gravel drive or path at the front of the house is a noisy surface that will alert you to the approach of visitors or intruders. For large areas, buy gravel in 1 tonne bulk bags which can be emptied straight onto the drive area on delivery. One tonne of gravel will cover about 16m² (19sq yd) at a depth of 25mm.

GETTING HELP FROM THE POLICE

If you want specific advice on how to protect your home, telephone the Crime Prevention Officer at your local police station. He will visit the house if necessary, point out weak spots in your defences and suggest the most appropriate security devices for your circumstances.

If you see anyone loitering in your street or acting suspiciously, do not disturb them. Call the police, then continue to watch unseen until they arrive.

Neighbourhood Watch groups, run in collaboration with the local police, are intended to encourage neighbours to work together by watching for anything suspicious in the area. They also stress the importance of protecting property, and marking valuables. If you are interested in getting involved in a group, contact your local Crime Prevention Officer.

9 Gates A gate at the garden boundary, particularly a locked one, is a very effective deterrent to burglars. To prevent a thief from lifting your gate off its hinges, drill a hole through one hinge pin and fit a small nut and bolt through it once the gate is hung.

10 Keys Never have a name-and-address tag on your keys. At most, use your surname, with a company address or the address of a relative for them to be returned to if you lose them. Be wary of leaving home to go and collect keys from someone who says they have found them. It may be a ruse to get you out of the house while the keys are used for entry. Never leave keys in locks, under the doormat, or hanging inside the letterbox.

Acknowledgments

All images in this book are copyright of the Reader's Digest Association Limited, with the exception of those in the following list.

The position of photographs and illustrations on each page is indicated by letters after the page number: **T** = Top; **B** = Bottom; **L** = Left; **R** = Right; **C** = Centre

58 B Clive Nichols/Joe Swift/Thamasin Marsh
91 TR, L, BR www.marshalls.co.uk
101 TL, TR, CR, BL www.marshalls.co.uk
118 BL www.screwfix.com
118 TR © RD/Debbie Patterson

Reader's Digest Outdoor and Garden DIY Manual is based on material in *Reader's Digest DIY Manual* and *1,001 DIY Hints and Tips*, both published by The Reader's Digest Association Limited, London

First Edition Copyright © 2006
The Reader's Digest Association Limited,
11 Westferry Circus, Canary Wharf,
London E14 4HE
www.readersdigest.co.uk

Editor Caroline Boucher
Art Editor Jane McKenna
Editorial Consultant Mike Lawrence
Proofreader Ron Pankhurst
Indexer Marie Lorimer

Reader's Digest General Books
Editorial Director Julian Browne
Art Director Nick Clark
Managing Editor Alastair Holmes
Head of Book Development Sarah Bloxham
Picture Resource Manager Martin Smith
Pre-press Account Manager Penny Grose
Senior Production Controller Deborah Trott
Product Production Manager Claudette Bramble

® Reader's Digest, The Digest and the Pegasus logo are registered trademarks of The Reader's Digest Association, Inc, of Pleasantville, New York, USA

The Reader's Digest Association Limited would like to thank the following organisations for the loan of tools, props and other materials for photographic shoots: Draper tools (www.drapertools.com)

Typesetting, illustration and photographic origination
Hardlines Limited, 17 Fenlock Court, Blenheim Office Park, Long Hanborough, Oxford OX29 8LN
Origination Colour Systems Limited, London
Printing and binding Everbest Printing Co Ltd, China

The contents of this book are believed to be accurate at the time of printing. However the publisher accepts no responsibility or liability for any work carried out in the absence of professional advice.

We are committed to both the quality of our products and the service we provide to our customers. We value your comments, so please feel free to contact us on 08705 113366, or via our website at www.readersdigest.co.uk
If you have any comments about the content of our books, email us at gbeditorial@readersdigest.co.uk

ISBN-13: 978 0276 44082 3
ISBN-10: 0 276 44082 X
BOOK CODE: 400-276-01
ORACLE CODE: 250007091H.00.24